DEBT RECOVERY TRIBUNALS

INTRODUCTION OF DRTS

ADV. PUSHPENDRA

INTRODUCTION

TO

DEBT

RECOVERY

TRIBUNALS

LIST OF ABBRIVETION

A.I.R. : All India Reporter

SCC : Supreme court cases

H.C.C : High court cases

HC. : High court

SC : Supreme court

CAPT. : Captain

e.g. : Example

I.P.C. : Indian Penal Code

Prof. : Professor

S. : Section

U.S.A. : United States of America

V. : Versus

i.e, : That is

ART : Article

TABLE OF CONTENT

CHAPTER – 1

INTROUDCTION DEFINITIONS

CHAPTER – 1

INTROUDCTION

"When men are pure, laws are useless; when men are corrupt, laws are broken" Benjamin Disraeli (1804-1881) British Politician and Author"

Money is the driving force behind all enterprises. It is the fountainhead of trade and commerce. When sufficient money is not available in the economy, it is not possible to promote any trade and commerce. A short term or long term assistance of finance to promote business is the need of the day. Banks in India provide short-term assistance, long term as well as mini term financial assistance for the growth of agricultural and industrial activities in the country. As a result of rapid growth in the industrial area, the role of banks has become very dynamic in achieving the highest levels of industrialization and developments in agriculture.

Before the Recovery of Debts Due to Banks and Financial Institutions Act, 1993 was placed in the Statute Book, banks had to institute a suit in a Court having civil jurisdiction for the recovery of debts due to banks and financial institutions. The way in which they had to recover the debts always took inordinate delay in settlement of their claims, as Civil Courts are flooded with cases for adjudication. This caused considerable difficulties in recovering the dues and enforcement of security due to the delay in the legal process. A significant portion of the funds of banks and financial institutions were thus blocked in unproductive assets, the value of which kept deteriorating with passage of time. The borrowers and guarantors were also facing difficulties due to the delay in delivering justice.

The legal procedures in existence prior to the year 1993 for recovery of debts due to banks and financial institutions, were time consuming, ineffective and had blocked a significant portion of the funds in unproductive assets. In 1981, a Committee under the Chairmanship of Shri.T. Tiwari had examined the legal and other difficulties faced by banks and suggested remedial measures including changes in the law. The Tiwari Committee had also suggested for setting up of special tribunals for recovery of dues to banks and financial institutions by following a summary procedure.

In the year 1991, the Committee on the Financial System constituted by the Central Government under the Chairmanship of Shri. M. Narasimhan recommended to the Government for setting up of Special Tribunals to expedite the recovery process. Accordingly, the Parliament enacted the Recovery of Debts Due to Banks and Financial Institutions Act, 1993 with the objective of providing for expeditious adjudication and recovery of debts due to banks and financial institutions through Debt Recovery Tribunal (DRT). The Act came into force on 24.06.1993. This Act intended to provide for expeditious adjudication and recovery of debts due to banks and financial institutions.

With the advent of the Recovery of Debts Due To Banks and Financial Institutions Act, 1993 (hereinafter referred to as DRT Act), it was expected that most of the Non Performing Assets (NPA) shall be easy to recover from defaulters. However, it was realised in due course that the enactment of DRT Act was not enough to fight the menace of the NPA's and deliver justice to the genuine borrowers/guarantors. With the object of giving more powers and skill to banks and delivering justice to the affected parties, the Government decided to bring in the Securitisation and Reconstruction of Financial Assets and Enforcement of Security Interest Act, 2002 (hereinafter referred to as SARFAESI Act).

During this period, there was pressure on the banks to achieve the international standards and the banks in India were progressively complying with the international prudential norms and standards. During this period, the banks in India have demanaded level playing fields with international banks. Prior to 2002, there was no provision for facilitating securitisation of financial assets and the power to take possession of securitized assets and selling them off.

The SARFAESI Act, 2002 has been enacted with an intention to strengthen the creditors rights through foreclosure and enforcement of securities by banks and financial institutions, by conferring on the creditors the right to seize the secured asset and sell the same in order to recover the dues promptly by passing over the costly and very time consuming legal process through Courts.

The legal framework in existence prior to the enactment of SARFAESI Act has not kept

pace with the changing commercial practices and financial sector reforms and it has resulted in a slow pace of recovery of defaulting loans and mounting levels of non-performing assets of banks

of and financial institutions. The Narasimhan Committee I and II and Andhyarujina Committee constituted by the Central Government for the purpose of examining banking sector reforms have considered the need for changes in the legal system in respect to these areas. These Committees, inter alia, have suggested enactment of a new legislation for securitisation and empowering banks and financial institutions to take possession of the securities and sell them without the intervention of the Court. Acting on these suggestions, the Securitisation and Reconstruction of Financial Assets and Enforcement of Security Interest Ordinance, 2002 was promulgated by the Central Government on 21st June 2002 to regulate securitisation and reconstruction of financial assets and enforcement of security interest and for matters connected therewith and incidental thereto. The Ordinance got the assent of the President and became an Act.

The SARFAESI Act has been enacted to enable banks to realize long-term assets, manage problem of liquidity, asset liability mismatches and improve recovery by exercising powers to take possession of securities, sell them and reduce non-performing assets by adopting the measures as stipulated under the provisiions of SARFAESI Act.

The SARFAESI Act, 2002 basically deals with four aspects:-

I.   Enforcement of Security Interest by secured creditor/banks.

I.   Transfer of non-performing assets to Asset Reconstruction Company, which will then dispose of those assets and realise the proceeds.

II.   To provide a legal framework for Securitisation of assets.

IV.   To provide for adjudication of grievances of the affected persons.

The Constitutional validity of the SARFAESI Act came under the consideration of the the Hon'ble Supreme Court of India in the popular case of Mardia Chemicals Ltd v. Union of India[1].

The Hon'ble Supreme Court of India upheld the validity of the Act and its provisions except that of sub-section (2) of Section 17 of the Act, which was declared ultra vires of Article 14 of the Constitution of India. It was also observed that where a secured creditor has taken action under

[1] AIR 2004 SC 2371

Section 13(4) of the Act, in such cases it would be open to borrowers / guarantors to file Appeals under Section 17 of the Act, within the limitation as prescribed.

The Origins of Debt Recovery Tribunals

Exhibit 1 gives the list of DRTs and DRATs. This section briefly traces their evolution and key episodes that led to their formation. Pre-DRT Resolution Process In India, banks and financial institutions had been required to institute a suit in civil court to proceed with recovery. The suit was tried and decided in accordance with the procedure laid down in Civil Procedure Code (CPC), 1908 (Dubey 2013). The CPC resolution process was long and cumbersome. In 1981, a committee under the Chairmanship of Mr. T. Tiwari was formed to suggest reforms. The committee observed that the Indian civil court system was burdened with diverse types of cases. Thus, recovery of dues due to banks and financial institutions was often not given priority. The committee suggested other modes to recover such dues. One measure was to set up quasi-judicial bodies to deal exclusively with the recovery process of the financial sector. These bodies could follow a faster "summary proceedings" process for disposing of cases. However, actual action on the formation of such bodies was not initiated until about a decade later around the Indian financial market and economic liberalization.

The 1993 RDDBFI Act

In 1991, the Committee on the Financial System headed by Shri M. Narasimham (Narasimham Committee I) endorsed the views of the Tiwari Committee and recommended setting up Special Tribunals (DRT Ernakulam website, accessed December 4, 2014). As backdrop for this recommendation, the committee noted the workload on the court system due to defaults. As of 30th September 1990, more than 1.5 million cases filed by the public sector banks and 304 cases filed by the financial institutions were pending in various courts. The recovery of debts involved more than ` 5,622 crore owed to public sector banks and ` 391 crores to other financial institutions.

The Narasimham committee recommendations led to the enactment of the Recovery of Debts Due to Banks and Financial Institutions Act (RDDBFI), 1993. The Act established two types of agencies, Debt Recovery Tribunals (DRTs) and Debt Recovery Appellate Tribunals (DRATs) and conferred upon them special powers for adjudication of debt recovery matters. Thus, the

earliest establishment of DRTs as institutional entities to resolve bankruptcy occurred in 1993. The first DRT was formed in Calcutta (now Kolkata) on 27th April 1994.

DRT Legitimacy Questions

Uncertainty about the legitimacy of DRTs continued for close to a half-decade. The constitutional validity of the RDDBFI Act was challenged before the Delhi High Court by the Delhi Bar Association. On March 10, 1995, the Delhi High Court ruled that the RDDBFI Act was unconstitutional because it compromised the independence of the judiciary from the executive. The Court found other anomalies. For instance, the Court ruled that lack of provisions for counter-claims by defendants made the Act biased towards the creditors conferring upon debt recovery the status of a tax (Dubey 2013). The national government moved the Supreme Court against the judgment. On March 18, 1996, the Supreme Court issued an interim order that, notwithstanding any stay order passed in any writ petition, DRTs should resume function. It also asked the central government to amend the law to address certain anomalies, which the government complied with in 2000. Subsequently the amendment made to the RDDBFI Act in 2000 allowed the defendant to make counter claims, and also strengthened the independence of DRTs from the executive branch of government.

In a final ruling on March 14, 2002, the Supreme Court stated that the RDDBFI Act with the amendments was constitutional. At this time all the pending cases about the constitutional validity of the act were dismissed (Visaria, 2009). Any residual questions about the legitimacy of the DRTs ended with the March 14, 2002 ruling.

Scope of DRTs and DRATs

Exhibit 1 shows that debt recovery tribunals were set up under the RDDBFI Act just after its passage. We next discuss what cases they can take up and what items the tribunals can rule on.

Entry into DRT

Formally, an application for recovery of debt can be made to the DRTs for all debts valued at more than INR 1 million.[2] For lesser amounts, the banks and financial institutions can avail

[2] Section 2(g) of the RDDBFI Act defines debt as any liability (inclusive of interest) which is claimed as due from any person by bank or a financial institution or by a consortium in cash or otherwise, whether secured or unsecured, or

normal remedy process such as the Civil Courts. The Act further authorizes the Central Government to specify such other amount, being not less than INR 1 lakh, that can be assigned to DRTs. This provision enables rationalization and coherence with other bankruptcy legislation such as SARFAESI that specify different amounts and that can also be taken up by DRT. In terms of process, Section 22 (1) of the Act is the operative portion. The Section states that the DRT and DRAT are to be guided by the principles of natural justice. They have powers to regulate their own procedure and in particular are not to be bound by the procedure laid down by the former CPC.

Operationally approach to the higher courts is through writ petitions filed at the courts. A law degree is not necessary to argue such cases.

Jurisdiction of DRTs

The jurisdictional powers and authority of the DRT and DRAT are set up so civil courts do not directly intervene on the main issue on which DRTs must rule. Section 17 of the RDDBFI Act vests in the DRT the authority to entertain applications from banks and financial institutions for recovery of debts due to such banks and financial institutions.[3] The DRAT has the power to address appeals made against any order made, or deemed to have been made, by the DRT. Section 18 of the Act bars all other Courts in relation to the matters of debt apart from the Supreme Court and High Court, whose authority flows from articles 226 and 227 of the Indian Constitution. The bottom line is that relief against a judgment of DRAT can be sought only from the High Court and the Supreme Court.

assigned, or whether payable under a decree or order of any civil court or any arbitration award or otherwise or under a mortgage and subsisting on, and legally recoverable on, the date of the application.

[3] Section 2(e) of the RDDBFI Act defines banks as (i) banking company; (ii) corresponding new bank(; iii) State Bank of India (iv) subsidiary bank (v) Regional Bank (vi) Multi state co-operative bank. Section 2(h) of the RDDBFI Act defines financial institution as (i) a public financial institution within the meaning of Section 4A of the Companies Act, 1956; (ii) such other institution as the Central Government may, having regard to its business activity and the area of its operation in India by notification, specify.

Interventions by Lower Courts Not Entirely Precluded

While the DRT process was designed to decongest lower courts, in practice, the lower courts do play a role in the DRT process because the judicial powers conferred by the RDDBFI Act on the DRT and DRAT are quite narrow. In the judgment of the Supreme Court in the suit of Standard Chartered Bank versus Dharmindar Bhoi and others (Civil Appeal 8486, 2013), the Court stressed that the DRT and DRAT can adjudicate on matters only in their domain as defined in section 17 of this Act. For instance, the DRTs and DRATs do not have jurisdiction on matters such as succession rights of property, monitoring and implementation of KYC norms or issuance of receipts. Such issues can and do arise during the debt recovery process, e.g., to infer security interest but the disputes on this issues can require rulings from civil courts that have a broader jurisdiction than the DRTs and DRATs. Thus, civil courts are approached for resolution on these matters even as they proceed through the DRT or DRAT, delaying DRT process pending guidance through decisions from Civil Courts.

The DRT process

Figure 1 provides a visual depiction of the entire DRT process. There are two routes to approach DRTs, through direct application or through the SARFAESI route. Figure 2 illustrates the SARFAESI route to DRT. We discuss these routes and the process forward for case disposal.

Application Route

The recovery procedure under this route is invoked by making an application to (and not filing a suit with) the DRT and paying the prescribed fees. What DRT location is chosen under this route is a good question. There are currently 32 DRTs in India in 22 unique locations. Some cities have multiple DRTs to deal with the inflow of large number of filings of applications. Section 19 of the RDDBFI Act specifies the conditions for choice of DRT to make an application. An application can be made by the bank or financial institution to a DRT that has jurisdiction in the region where the defendant (one or more defendants, if more than one) actually or voluntarily resides, or carries business. An application may also be filed to a particular DRT if the cause of action wholly or in part arises within the limits of its jurisdiction.

SARFAESI Route

An application can also be made to the DRT under the Securitisation and Reconstruction for Enforcement of Security Interest Act (SARFAESI), 2002. Before discussing this point further, it is useful to briefly summarize the SARFAESI Act. Like the DRT process, the SARFAESI Act was also based on the recommendations of committees, specifically the Narasimham Committee

– II (1998) and the Andhyarujina Committee (1999). These committees recognized the need to strengthen the rights of secured creditors to assist them in recovering their dues. SARFAESI sets out the process for doing so without the intervention of courts or tribunals.

The SARFAESI process is as follows. Under section 13 (2) of the SARFAESI Act, after a loan has been classified as a non-performing asset (NPA) by the secured creditor, a notice to this effect is sent to the relevant borrower. This notice must clearly mention the outstanding amount to be repaid in full within a period of 60 days by the borrower, failing which the secured creditor is entitled to exercise the rights in accordance with section 13 (4) of the Act. While the initial versions of the Act gave borrowers no rights to appeal against this notice, a later version introduced Sub-section 3A into SARFAESI Act to allow borrower appeals against 13(2) notices.[4] This appeal can be made to the secured creditor alone. The bank is expected to respond to the appeal of the borrower within fifteen days. If the borrower is unable to discharge his liabilities, sub-section 4 of section 13 of the Act authorizes the secured creditor to take recourse to measures of recovery by taking possession of the secured asset including the right to transfer by way of lease, assignment or sale, take over management of the business or appoint any person to manage the secured asset.

The transition into DRTs occurs when collateral is insufficient to fulfill obligations to creditors. In such instances where dues of the secured creditors are not fully satisfied with the sale proceeds of the secured assets, the creditors may file an application to the DRT for recovery of the remaining portion of the dues. The borrower can also appeal to the DRT against the creditor's findings.[5]

[4] The amendment was motivated by the observations made by the Supreme Court in Mardia Chemicals vs. Union of India (AIR 2004 SC 2371).

[5] Per Section 17 of the SARFAESI Act, borrowers can appeal against any action taken by the creditor under section 13 (4).

Prior to 2004, transitions from SARFAESI into DRTs were extremely costly for borrowers. An appeal could be made to the DRT by the borrower only after depositing 75% of the amount specified in the notice issued under section 13(2). At the discretion of the DRT this amount could be reduced or waived. This is particularly punitive for distressed borrowers who by definition lack resources. Asking them to deposit a further 75% of the claimed amount is costly. It may, paradoxically, be raised yet again from the banking system itself. The 2004 amendments permits appeal to the DRT by paying only the fees prescribed by the RDDBFI Act, which are applicable to all applications made to the DRT.

Post Filing: DRT Process

To expedite court processes, adjudication by DRTs and DRATs is by summary proceeding. The powers of the tribunal are quite substantial. Section 19 (12) of the Act empowers the DRT to make an interim order against the defendant to debar him from disposing or transferring any property and assets belonging to him without prior permission of the Tribunal. It also has the power to detain the defendant for a maximum of three months for disobedience of an order or breach of any terms of an order issued under sections 19(12), 19(13) and 19(18) of the SARFAESI Act.

In the direct application route, the recommended time to completion is 180 days from the receipt of the application as per Sections 19(4) of RDDBFI. For applications made to DRT under the SARFAESI Act, DRTs are asked to dispose cases within 60 days, with an outer limit of 4 months. If the period exceeds 4 months section 17(6) of the SARFAESI Act entitles either party to the application to make an application to the DRAT to direct the DRT for disposal of the pending application.

The submission of an application to the DRT triggers, summons issued to the defendant requiring him to show cause within 30 days as to why relief prayed for should not be granted. The defendant must present a written statement. The Tribunal may permit additional time for submission of this statement. The defendant can plead a set-off against any ascertained sum of money legally recoverable by him from the applicant at the first hearing and not afterwards unless permitted by the Tribunal. A counter-claim against the claim of the applicant can be made by the applicant before delivering his defense.

On the basis of the DRT's order, the Presiding Officer of the DRT issues a certificate to the Recovery Officer for recovery of the amount of debt specified in the certificate. The Recovery officer can recover dues by attaching, selling and appointing a receiver for the management of the defendants' property. The DRTs can also obtain a police warrant to arrest the defendant (Visaria, 2009).

Post-Filing: DRAT

An appeal against the order of the DRT can be made to the DRAT within whose jurisdiction the DRT falls. There are currently 5 DRATs in Mumbai, Delhi, Kolkata, Chennai, and Allahabad. The appeal has to be made within a period of 45 days from the order of the DRT, which may be extended by the DRAT. Additionally, the DRAT can be approached for interim relief on interim applications (IA) or miscellaneous applications (MA) which are sub-sections of the original applications.

Appeals to DRAT can be expensive. The aggrieved party that owes the debt must deposit 75% of the amount determined by the order of the DRT. This amount can be reduced or waived by the DRAT. For appeals to DRAT that originate in the SARFAESI Act actions, the deposit is 50% of the amount which is claimed by the secured creditor or the amount as determined in the order of DRT or the, whichever is less. However an important point is that unlike applications under RDDBFI, the deposits cannot be fully waived but only be reduced to 25% of the amount.

Inefficiencies in the Actual Recovery Process

Informal discussions with industry reveal that the recovery process is inefficient and often witnesses lack of robust participation in properties auctioned under DRTs. A key issue is the presence of claw back provisions as discussed below.

Under the DRT, a bank recovers its dues by sale of the asset by publicly auctioning it. It is mandatory for the bank to advertise the auction in the leading newspapers, after mentioning a reserve price. One day is allotted to the potential buyers to examine the asset and verify its documents.

Bidders must deposit a refundable amount called the earnest money deposit (EMD), which could be 15% of the reserve price. Upon winning the auction the successful bidder has to pay the

remaining amount within the period determined by the bank. If the bidder is unwilling or unable to pay the remaining amount, the EMD is not refunded. Following the successful bidding of the asset a 30 day cooling period is observed. During this period, an injunction may be sought. For instance, the owner of the asset may argue that the price is lower than expected or there may be lack of proper advertising of the asset. Other bidders could contest the auction on grounds that the bank did not furnish sufficient documents during inspection of the property.

The bank may re-auction the asset if it does not get the expected price for it. Less frequently, banks may choose to settle for a price that is lower than the reserve price. Informal discussions suggest that the illiquidity of the asset and the specificity in value of the asset to the original borrower can result in peculiar outcomes. For instance, the original owner of the property may have the highest value of the asset, in which case the debt is effectively reduced to the valuation of the asset to the defaulter, who then has the option of purchasing a property back at price that is lesser than what is originally due under the defaulted loan. These types of inefficiencies can arise in many bankruptcy proceedings and are thus clearly not unique to DRTs or India. However, protracted proceedings in the legal bankruptcy process offer more opportunities for such situations to arise.

Interaction between SICA and RDDBFI Act

The Sick Industrial Companies Act (SICA), enacted in 1985, is an alternative channel to address financial distress faced by public[6] and private sector entities. As we discuss below, the process has relatively noble aims of avoiding liquidation in favor of restructuring. However, it has effectively become so pro-debtor that any restructuring is only a restructuring in name and lets owners continue to be in possession of assets for a long period of time. Thus, defaulters are given a long-lived options on the asset even if it is in distress. The resultant heads-I-win tails-you-lose situation is a recipe for excessive risk-taking and non-resolution of distress.

Under SICA, a company is defined as 'sick' in section 3(o) of SICA, if at the end of any financial year the accumulated accounting losses equal to or exceed its entire net worth6[7]. A potentially sick company is one whose losses have eroded by 50% or more of its peak net worth

[6] Government Company as defined by section 617 of Company Act 1956 came under purview of SICA, due to amendments made in 1991.

[7] Section 3(h) of SICA defines net worth as the sum total of the paid-up capital and free reserves.

during the immediately four financial years. Such firms may also seek rehabilitation under SICA. The Act serves firms in scheduled industries as annexed in the First Schedule of the Industrial Development Regulation Act, 1951 (IDRA). Provisions of SICA are applicable only to those companies that have completed five years since their registration[8] and which have 50 or more workers on any day of the 12 months preceding the end of the financial year with reference to which sickness is claimed.[9]

SICA established the quasi-judicial bodies of Board for Industrial and Financial Reconstruction (BIFR) and the Appellate Authority for Industrial and Financial Reconstruction (AAIFR). The bodies have sweeping powers through Section 22 of SICA, which overrides and stops all other legal contracts and proceedings while an inquiry is pending with the BIFR or AAIFR. Contracts stop even if any scheme is under preparation, consideration, or under implementation under SICA. If so, no action can be taken by creditors for recovery without prior approval of BIFR or AAIFR. While the intent of the provision is to preserve assets during the proceedings in the BIFR, they can also be used by promoters to stop all actions taken by creditors. This provision as given in section 22 is a main reason for the failure of SICA to resolve distress.

SICA can dilute the force of debt recovery tribunals. Section 34 of RDDBFI clearly states that the provisions of the Act defining the scope of DRTs are in addition and not in derogation of the SICA. Thus companies can approach BIFR even after an application has been filed by their creditors in the DRT, which effectively stalls recovery proceedings cleared by DRTs. The enactment of SARFAESI Act presented a partial remedy to this problem. Section 15 of SICA provides that a reference made to BIFR shall abate if secured creditors representing not less than 60% in value of the amount outstanding take measures to enforce the security as per the provisions of SARFAESI Act. Thus, firms can be pulled out of BIFR, potentially irreversibly, through actions under SARFAESI as secured creditors. Once outside the BIFR section 22 of SICA is not applicable to the company. Any appeal made against this enforcement under SARFAESI is, at least in principle, the domain of DRTs. Not surprisingly, SARFAESI remains the most pro-creditor tool of choice in debt enforcement.

[8] New ventures effectively have a moratorium period of five years before being declared sick.

[9] For instance, ancillary and small scale industrial undertakings as defined in section 3 of IDRA do not come under the purview of this Act. This was specifically done so that focus remains on rescuing companies that are of Economic importance.

DEFINITIONS

Many concepts discussed and analysed in this research and definitions given for those concepts are sepcific only for this study. In terms of Section 2(1) (c) of the SARFAESI Act, "bank" means

-

(i) a banking company or i. a corresponding new bank or

iii.   the State Bank of India or

iv.   a subsidiary bank or

v.   a multi-state co-operative bank or

vi.   such other bank which the Central Government may, by notification, specify for the purposes of this Act.

The definition of bank as given under Section 2(1)(c) is wider in scope. The word "bank" used in this study refers to the banking company as defined under Section 5(c) of the Banking Regulation Act, 1949.

In terms of Section 2(1)(f) of SARFAESI Act, "borrower" means any person who has been granted financial assistance by any bank or finanacial institution or who has given any guarantee or created any mortgage or pledge as security for the finanacial assistance granted by any bank or financial institution and includes a person who becomes borrower of a securitization company or reconstruction company consequent upon acquisition by it of any rights or interest of any bank or financial institution in relation to such financial assistance.

The definition of borrower as given under Section 2(1)(f) is wider in scope. The word "borrower" used in this study refers to borrower and guarantor as specified in the business of banking.

In terms of Section 2(i)(k) of the SARFAESI Act, financial assistance means any loan or advance granted or any debentures or bonds subscribed or any guarantees given or letters of credit established or any other credit facility extended by any bank of financial institution. The

term financial assistance in this study refers only to loans or advances extended by banks to borrowers and guarantors.

In terms of Section 2(1)(o) of SARFAESI Act, "non-performing asset" means an asset or account of a borrower, which has been classified by a bank of financial institution as sub- standard [doubtful] or lost asset-

a. in case such bank or financial institution is administered or regulated by any authority or body established, constituted or appointed by any law for the time being in force, in accordance with the directions or guidelines relating to assets classification issued by such authority or body;

b. in any other case, in accordance with the directions or guidelines relating to assets classifications issued by the Reserve Bank.

In this study, "non-performing asset" means the asset or account of a borrower classified by a bank in accordance with the directions or guidelines of Reserve Bank of India.

In terms of Section 2(1)(zd) "secured creditor" means any bank or financial institution or any consortium or group of banks or financial institutions and includes-

i. debenture trustee appointed by any bank or financial institution or

ii. securitisation company or reconstruction company, whether acting as such or managing a trust set up by such securitisation company or reconstruction compnay for the securitisation or reconstruction, as the case may be or

iii. any other trustee holding securities on behalf of a bank or financial institution, in whose favour security interest is created for due repayment by any borrower of any financial assistance. The term secured creditor in this study refers only banks.

OBJECTIVES

Objectives of the study are based on the research questions and are listed out as follows:-

1. To conduct a juristic analysis of the issues and challenges in implementation of the provisions of SARFAESI Act, 2002.
2. To test the changing trends in the process of recovery laws adopted and implemented by Banks for recovery of dues.
3. To study the difficulties and hardships faced by borrowers and guarantors while dealing with the provisions of the SARFAESI Act.

iv.   To suggest legal measures to strengthen the provisions of the SARFAESI Act, 2002 in the context of new economic order.

HYPOTHESES

The primary object of this study is to conduct a juristic analysis of the issues and challenges in implementation of the provisions of the SARFAESI Act, 2002 and to suggest legal measures to strengthen the provisions of the Securitisation and Reconstruction of Financial Assets and Enforcement of Security Interest Act, 2002. The following hypothesis are formulated for the purpose of the study:-

1. Inspite of the enactment of SARFAESI Act, 2002, the legal procedures for recovery of dues are cumbersome, time consuming and non-delivering justice to Banks and

    Borrowers/Guarantors.

2. The provisions in the SARFAESI Act, 2002 are inadequate to redress the grievances of the affected borrowers and guarantors.
3. The prevailing provisions in the SARFAESI Act, 2002 are inadequate to address the post- implementation issues and challenges

RESEARCH PROBLEM

In the Tiwari Committee Report of 1981, it was stated in Chapter VIII, para.8.23 that in respect of suits by banks and financial institutions there have been abnormal delays at the stage of trial as well as the stage of execution in various courts and hence it stated:

"the principle that the State should have a special procedure to enforce its own demandsshould equally be extended to the recovery of dues of banks and financial institutions as well"[10].

The Committee recommended that a Tribunal under Arts.323-A and 323-B of the Constitution should be constituted. The Committee further recommended that the Tribunal should not be bogged down by the Code of Civil Procedure, 1908, but should have a simple procedure guided only by principles of natural justice.

The DRT Act, 1993 was enacted with an object to provide for expeditious adjudication and recovery of debts due to Banks and Financial Institutions through DRT. However, the Debt Recovery Tribunals constituted under the provisions of DRT Act, 1993 was not so successful in recovering the bad debts due to banks and financial institutions as the recovery procedures in DRT entangled in time consuming legal procedures and further banks did not have the required powers and skill to enforce the securities without approaching the Courts.

The backlogs and delays in adjudication of the cases before the Debt Recovery Tribunals have prompted the Central Government to examine the need for changes in the legal system. The Committees constituted by the Central Govt such as Narasimhan Committee and Andhyarujina Committee have suggested enactment of a new legislation for empowering banks to take possession of the securities and sell them without the intervention of the court. Acting on these suggestions, the Securitisation and Reconstruction of Financial Assets and Enforcement of Security Interest Act, 2002 was enacted by the Central Government.

The Civil Courts and Debt Recovery Tribunals have no doubt been efficient and successful to an extent in passing judgments recovering dues to banks and financial institutions delivering justice to borrowers/guarantors, but due to the inherent delay & time consuming legal processes, it failed to achieve its objects in full. Thereafter, the SARFAESI Act was passed in 2002. Now,

[10] Tiwari Committee Report of 1981, Chapter VIII, para.8.23

thirteen years have passed by after the enactment of the SARFAESI Act and it is time to look back and conduct a juristic analysis of the issues and challenges in implementation of the SARFAESI Act, 2002. This study will also suggest the measures to strengthen the provisions in the existing recovery laws for effective recovery.

The moot problems which the researcher endeavors to solve is as follows:-

1. What are the issues and challenges which arosed out of the implementation of the provisions of the SARFAESI Act ?
2. Whether the recovery laws, specifically the Securitisation and Reconstruction of Financial

Assets and Enforcement of Security Interest Act, 2002 (SARFAESI Act) are successful in delivering justice to banks and borrowers/guarantors ?

3. Whether the recovery laws, in particular the Securitisation and Reconstruction of Financial

Assets and Enforcement of Security Interest Act, 2002 (SARFAESI Act) are efficient enough to address the grievances of borrowers/guarantors of Bank's ?

4. Whether there is scope for improvement in the scheme or provisions of the SARFAESI Act?

If so, the measures to be suggested for enhancing the existing legal frame work ?

RESEARCH METHODOLOGY

The present study will be concentrated on the examination of the efficacy of recovery laws relating to Banks and Financial Institutions with special emphasis on Civil Courts, Debt Recovery Tribunals. Thirteen years have passed since the enactment of the Securitisation and Reconstruction of Financial Assets and Enforcement of Security Interest Act and therefore the present study will be concentrated on the juristic examination of the issues and challenges in implementation of the SARFAESI Act, 2015. This study will also suggest measures to strength the provisions in the existing recovery laws for delivering justice to all stake holders.

To substantiate the present study all the relevant reports of Law Commission, recommendations of different Committees on the subject, rules and regulations issued by the Ministry of Finance, RBI, will also be studied.

This research is partly doctrinal and non-doctrinal (emphrcal). In this research work, the doctrinal method of research, historical method of research and empirical method with random sampling technique are followed. In the historical method of research, the evolution and concept of recovery of debts by banks and the laws of the land and the evolution of the SARFAESI Act are discussed in length to know the origin and background.

In the doctrinal method of research, the statutory provisions of the Recovery of Debts Due to Banks and Financial Institutions Act and the Securitisation and Reconstruction of Financial Assets and Enforcement of Security Interest Act, 2002 are interpreted and analysed. The existing case laws with regard to the provisions have also been interpreted.

The empirical part of research consists of studies conducted by circulating questionnaires with multiple choice questions to the respondent borrowers, officials of banks, judicial officers, advocates, general public and data collected from them. The respondents were selected by following the simple random sampling technique for the study. The data collected from the respondents have been analyzed using SPSS (Statistical Package for Social Sciences) for achieving precision of measurement. Based on the analytical study conducted on the existing legal provisions with regard to the rights of banks and borrowers / guarantors and the findings obtained from the empirical study, an attempt has been made to test the research hypothesis and arrive at suggestions and recommendations.

It explores, analysis, formulates and compare the efficacy of various provisions of the SARFAESI Act vis-a-vis with the practical problems and bottlenecks faced and suffered by various constituents involved in the implementation of the SARFAESI Act.

Research progress by the following stages:-

- In the first stage, formulate and analyse the evolution and development of recovery laws with respect to the recovery of dues to banks.

- In the second stage, examine and analyse the various Indian Statutes wherein the concepts & measures for recovering dues to banks have been incorporated.
- In the third stage, the role of judiciary in interpreting and establishing recovery laws relating to banking institutions will be analysed.
- The fourth stage explores and examines the issues and challenges in enforcing the SARFAESI Act.
- In fifth stage, the perception, experience and suggestions of various stake holders towards the SARFAESI Act will be examined.
- In the final stage, in the light of various judgements and also the challenges faced by stake holders in the implementation of the SARFAESI Act, a juristic analysis of the provisions of the SARFAESI Act will be conducted and recommendation to plug the loopholes and improve the legal system will be suggested.

SOURCE OF DATA

In order to realise the objective of the study, materials from both primary and secondary sources have been collected and the information relevant to the research culled out, sifted and incorporated in the study wherever found necessary. The source materials have been taken from the Constitution of India, the Recovery of Debts Due to Banks and Financial Institutions Act 1993, Securitisation and Reconstruction of Financial Assets and Enforcement of Security Interest Act, 2002, statutory enactments, journals such as the All India Reporter, Supreme Court Cases, notifications from Reserve Bank of India and Ministry of Finance, Debt Recovery Tribunal Cases, Current Tamil Nadu cases as primary source. The speeches of legal luminaries, research papers of scholars, various text books, several surveys conducted earlier and information collected from different websites are utilised as secondary sources in the research.

CHAPTER - 2

REVIEW OF LITERATURE

There are multitudinous books and research articles dealing with Non Performing Assets in Bank and SARFAESI Act. The Srivastava's "Securitisation Debt & Recovery Laws along with allied Acts & Rules" 6th Edition deals with various provisions of the SARFAESI Act& DRT Act with judgements. However, the work of Srivastava essentially does not deal with the issues and challenges in implementation of the SARFAESI Act nor makes any suggestion for the improvement in the scheme of the Act.

Recently, Shri. M.R.Umarji has come up with 6th Edition on "Law & Practice Relating to Securitisation & Reconstruction of Financial Assets & Enforcement of Security Interest". This handbook details the various circulars, guidelines of RBI along with the provisions of SARFAESI & DRT Act. Further, it covers topics such as code of bank's commitments to customers, guidelines on fair practices code for lenders, prudential norms on income recognition, framework for revitalizing distressed assets, income recognition, asset classification provision, etc. However, this book also does not evaluate & examine the impact & effectiveness of the provisions of the SARFAESI Act from the standpoint of problems faced by the bankers, borrowers and the general public while implementing the provisions of the Act.

Prashanth K Reddy of the Indian Institute of Management Ahmedabad in his paper "A

Comparative study of Non Performing Assets in India in the Global Context - similarities and disminilarities, remedial measures"[11] observed that the problem of non-performing assets faced by banks in India is not due to lack of strict prudential norms but partly due to the legal impediments and time consuming nature of asset disposal process. The author is of the view that the introduction of SARFAESI Act has given wide ranging powers for banks to dispose off assets and allowed creation of Asset Reconstruction Companies. This paper basically examines the reasons for the growth of Non Performing Assets from a banking perspective. However, this paper does not examine the post implementation issues and challenges of SARFAESI Act.

[11]www.iimahd.ernet.in (accessed on 12/12/2014)

Meenakshi Rajeev and H.P. Mahesh of the Institute for Social and Economic Change, Bangalore in their work "Banking Sector Reforms and NPA: A study of Indian Commercial Banks"[12] examined the trends of Non Performing Assets in Indian Commercial Banks space from various dimensions. In their report it is stated that in India, due to the social banking motto, the problem of bad loans did not receive priority from policy makers, initially. However, with the reform of the financial sector and the adoption of international banking practices, the issue of NPA's received due focus. Thus, in India, the concept of NPA came into the reckoning after reforms in the financial sector were introduced on the recommendations of the Report of the Committee on the financial system (Narasimhan, 1991) and an appropriate accounting system was put in place. The authors summarised in their work that Non Performing Assets is the root cause of the global financial crisis and the world is still trying to recover from the after-effects of the crisis. Though this report deals extensively with the various dimensions of NPA, it does not discuss about the problems faced by the borrowers due to the implementation of SARFAESI Act.

Meenakshi Rajeev and H.P. Mahesh of the Institute for Social and Economic Change, Bangalore in their work "Banking Sector Reforms and NPA: A study of Indian Commercial Banks"3 examined the trends of Non Performing Assets in Indian Commercial Banks space from various dimensions. In their report it is stated that in India, due to the social banking motto, the problem of bad loans did not receive priority from policy makers, initially. However, with the reform of the financial sector and the adoption of international banking practices, the issue of NPA's received due focus. Thus, in India, the concept of NPA came into the reckoning after reforms in the financial sector were introduced on the recommendations of the Report of the Committee on the financial system (Narasimhan, 1991) and an appropriate accounting system was put in place. The authors summarised in their work that Non Performing Assets is the root cause of the global financial crisis and the world is still trying to recover from the after-effects of the crisis. Though this report deals extensively with the various dimensions of NPA, it does not discuss about the problems faced by the borrowers due to the implementation of SARFAESI Act.

All the works as discussed above either deals with the Non-Performing Assets in Banks or deals with various recovery laws such as the DRT Act and the SARFAESI Act. But no evocative work has been carried out to analyse the issues and challenges in implementation of the SARFAESI

[12] www.isec.ac.in (accessed on 15/10/2014)

Act from a juristice point of view. Therefore, the researcher has undertaken a partly doctrinal and partly non-doctrinal research work on the said subject.

CHAPTER – 3

THE EVOLUTION AND DEVELOPMENT OF RECOVERY LAWS RELATING TO BANKS AND FINANCIAL INSTITUTIONS

"Law and order exist for the purpose of establishing justice and when they fail in this purpose they become the dangerously structured dams that block the flow of social progress"

Martin Luther King Jr. (1929-1968) American black leader

Banking at all times, revolve around the concept of 'lending of money', and it is the main contributor of profit and the very source of income for the existnce of the banks. When we talk about advances by Banks, generally it takes the following three forms[13]:-

1. Cash Credit

2. Overdrafts

3. Loans

In simple banking parlance, a 'cash credit' is an arrangement by a Bank made to its customer to borrow money up to a certain limit against the values of his stocks and book debts for his day to day requirement. The term 'overdraft' is a temporary accommodation allowed to a customer to overdraw his current account, usually against collateral securities. 'Loans' generally means advances made by a banker in a lump sum, the whole of which is withdrawn and is supposed to be repaid generally wholly at any time.

The Banks are extending credit facilities to borrowers under the agreement that the same will be repaid as per the schedule and on repayment, the same shall be circulated among the general public who are in need of cash. However, when the money granted by Banks failed to return back, the Banks will face the situation of out of funds and ultimately it will result in failure of credit facilities to the needy persons in the society and also adversely affect the growth of the economy.

This vicious circle has got far reaching consequences and in due course, the health of the country's economy will also be in stake. While analysing the rights of Bankers vis-a-vis the duty cast upon the borrowers to repay the dues, it can safely conclude that the Bankers right to recover their dues are of paramount importance. However, the Bankers right to recovery of dues from the borrowers/guarantors shall be strictly guided by the provisisions of the applicable laws.

So, recovery of money from defaulted borrowers through various legal recourse is a matter of large importance for Bankers from the very first day of its business. However, it is equally important that the legal measures excercised by Banks are in confirmity with the pricniples of natural justice and not in violation of the rights guaranteed to the borrowers/guarantors under the various provisoions of the law inforce.

In Banking pralance, the concept of 'recovery of dues' from the borrowers/guarantors has got two phases. The first phase is termed as 'soft recovery', wherein the Bankers used to adopt the soft techinques for recovery of dues such as issuing letters to borrowers, meeting them in person, visit to their residence or place of business or office, etc. In this stage, the Bankers are not adopting the strict enforcement of legal provisions, but pursuing the borrowers/guarantors to repay their dues without resorting to the legal proceedings. In the second phase, the Bankers are resorting to the enforcement of legal proceedings before the appropriate judicial forum for adjudication of their dues.

I. DIFFERENT STAGES OF EVOLUTION OF RECOVERY LAWS

In this context, it was decided to examine how the recovery laws pertaining to Banking have been evolved and developed over the period of time. For the purpose of this research, the evolution and development of the recovery laws relating to Banking Institutions has been divided into three stages. The recovery laws specific to Banking have undergone the following phases/stages in its long journey:-

Period up to the enactment of the Recovery of Debts Due to Banks and Financial Institutions Act, 1993, it is called as 'Pre-DRT Stage'.

- Period from the enactment of the Recovery of Debts Due to Banks and Financial Institutions Act, 1993 up to the enactment of the Securitisation and Reconstruction of Financial Assets and Enforcement of Security Interest Act, 2002, it is termed as 'DRT Stage'.
- Period from the enactment of the Securitisation and Reconstruction of Financial Assets and Enforcement of Security Interest Act, 2002 and thereafter, it is named as 'Sarfaesi Stage'.

In terms of Section 67 of the Transfer of Property Act, the mortgagee has, at any time after the mortgage money has become due to him and before a decree has been made for the redemption of the mortgaged property or the mortgage-money has been paid or deposited, has got right to obtain from the court a decree that the mortgagor shall be absolutely debarred of his right to redeem the property or a decree that the property be sold.

In the first stage of evolution Pre-DRT Stage i.e. period up to the enactment of the Recovery of Debts Due to Banks and Financial Institutions Act, 1993, the Bankers were required to file all suits for recovery of money before the concerned Courts with civil jurisdiction. Since, the civil courts are burdened with large amount of cases, the suits filed by Banks also got delayed and Bankers used to receive decree after waiting for considerable period of time say 3 to 5 years. Due to the long delay in getting the decree, instances of security being diluted and disposal of security by the borrowers became very common. Further, the usual procedures adopted in civil courts have also contributed in delaying the award of decrees in cases filed by Banks.

The Committee on the Financial System constituted by the Government of India under the Chairmanship of Shri.M.Narasimhan considered the setting up of the Special Tribunals for adjudication of recovery cases of banks with special powers for adjudication and speedy recovery and made observation that setting up of such Special Tribunals are critical to the successful implementation of the financial sector reforms. An urgent need was, therefore, felt by the Union of Govt. of India to work out a suitable mechanism through which the dues to the banks and financial

institutions could be realized without delay. In 1981, a Committee under the Chairmanship of Shri. T.Tiwari was also examined the legal and other difficulties faced by banks and financial institutions and suggested remedial measures including changes in law. The Tiwari Committee also suggested setting up of Special Tribunals for recovery of dues of the banks and financial

institutions by following a summary procedure. It was felt that setting up of Special Tribunals will not only fulfill a long-felt need, but also will be an important step in the implementation of the Report of Narasimham Committee. As per the data available on 30th September, 1990 more than fifteen lakh of cases filed by the public sector banks and about 304 cases filed by the financial institutions were pending in various courts and more than Rs.5622 crores in dues of Public Sector Banks and about Rs.391 crores in dues of the financial institutions were involved.in these cases. The locking up of such huge amount of public money in litigation in this way prevented proper utilization and recycling of the funds for the development of the country.

The account/asset which turned into bad debt due to non-payment of principal or interest which in banking terminology means "Non-Performing Assets" (hereinafter referred to as 'NPA') beyond a certain level are indeed a cause for concern for all stake holders in financial sector, because the availability of credit is essential for economic growth of the country and accumulation of NPAs affect the smooth flow of credit. Though the inability/incapacity of the genuine borrowers/guarantors to repay the dues is an issue for the Banks to find a solution, the right of the Banks to recovery dues from defaulted borrowers/guarantors can't be a ground for justification of dealy or deficicency in recovery procedings. The Banks raises resources not just on fresh deposits, but also by recycling the funds received from the borrowers. Thus, when a loan becomes nonperforming, it affects the entire recycling of credit and credit creation.[14]

It is a fact that the financial sector is playing a pivotal role in India's efforts to achieve success in progressively developing its economy. While the Banking sector in India is making efforts to comply with the international prudential norms and accounting practices, the Banking sector is holding the view that there are certain areas in which the Indian banking and financial sector do not have a level playing field as compared to other participants in the financial markets in the world. The Indian Banking sector also hold the view that there was no legal provision in existence prior to the enactment of the SARFAESI Act, for facilitating securitization of financial assets of banks and financial institutions.

[14] Banking sector reforms and NPA: A study of Indian Commercial Banks-working paper by Meenakshi Rajeev and H P Mahesh-Institute for Social and Economic Change, Bangalore.

The Tiwari Committee in its report of 1981, stated in Chapter VIII, para.8.23 that in respect of suits by banks and financial institutions there have been abnormal delays at the stage of trial as well as at the stage of execution in various courts and hence it stated:

"The principle that the State should have a special procedure to enforce its own demands should equally be extended to the recovery of dues of banks and financial institutions as well".

On a closer scrutiny, the recommendation of the Tiwar Committee has got relevance on the follwing points:-

1. The Committee emphasized the constitution of the Tribunal on the same principle as that of a State, where a State has got a special procedure to enforce its own demands, the bankers should have a Special Tribunal to enforce its dues.
2. The committee recommended that a Tribunal under Arts.323-A and 323-B of the constitution should be constituted.
3. The committee further recommended that the Tribunal should not bogged down by the Code of Civil Procedure, 1908 but should have a simple procedure guided only by principles of natural justice.

I (A). THE EVOLUTION OF THE RECOVERY LAWS – PRE DRT STAGE

In the Pre-DRT stage, the Banks were filing suits before the competent courts under Section 26 and Order VII Rule I of the Code of Civil Procedure for recovery of the dues. These suits were adjudicated by the competent courts at par with other cases filed before the concerned court. Since the suits filed by Banks didn't receive any preferences, it took years to get the decree. Further, the execution petition filed in pursuance of the decree also took its own time to complete the process.

Since the Banks are involved in distribution of public money for the development of the social and economic features of the country, the blocking of large amount of money in lengthy litigation has adversely affected the interest of the country. In these given circumstances, the Banks demanded a separate tribunal for adjudication of their claim.

The statement of objects and reasons[15] of the Recovery of Debts Due to Banks and Financial Institutions Act, 1993 reflects the concern of the India Parliament towards the difficulties faced by Banks& Financial Institutions in recovering loans and enforcement of securities charged with them. The Parliament in the statement of objects of the Act has admitted that the existing procedure for recovery of debts due to the banks and financial institutions has blocked a significant portion of their funds in unproductive assets, the value of which deteriorates with the passage of time.

I(B). ENACTMENT OF THE RECOVERY OF DEBTS DUE TO BANKS AND FINANCIAL INSTITUTIONS ACT, 1993 -DRT STAGE

30-09-1990 more than 15 lakh cases filed by public sector banks and 304 cases filed by financial institutions were pending in various courts for recovery of debts, etc. amounting to Rs.6000 crores, the Parliament enacted the Recovery of Debts Due to Banks and Financial Institutions Act, 1993(DRT Act). The new legislation facilitated creation of specialized forums i.e., the Debts Recovery Tribunals and the Debts Recovery Appellate Tribunals for expeditious adjudication of disputes relating to recovery of the debts due to banks and financial institutions. Simultaneously, the jurisdiction of the Civil Courts was barred and all pending matters were transferred to the Tribunals from the date of their establishment.

An analysis of the provisions of the DRT Act shows that primary object of that Act was to facilitate creation of special machinery for speedy recovery of the dues of banks and financial institutions. This is the reason why the DRT Act not only provides for establishment of the Tribunals and the Appellate Tribunals with the jurisdiction, powers and authority to make summary adjudication of applications made by banks or financial institutions and specifies the modes of recovery of the amount determined by the Tribunal or the Appellate Tribunal but also bars the jurisdiction of all courts except the Supreme Court and the High Courts in relation to the matters specified in Section 17. The Tribunals and the Appellate Tribunals have also been freed from the shackles of procedure contained in the Code of Civil Procedure. To put it differently, the DRT Act has not only brought into existence special procedural mechanism for speedy recovery of the dues of banks and financial institutions, but also made provision for ensuring that

[15] Statement of objects and reasons of the Recovery of Debts due to Banks and Financial Institutions Act, 1993 (Act No.51 of 1993)

defaulting borrowers are not able to invoke the jurisdiction of Civil Courts for frustrating the proceedings initiated by the banks and other financial institutions.

The Recovery of Debts due to Banks and Financial Institutions Act, 1993 was enacted with an object to provide for expeditious adjudication and recovery of debts due to Banks and Financial Institutions through Debt Recovery Tribunal (DRT) and Debt Recovery Appellate Tribunal (DRAT). The DRT's had problems in starting to function effectively but the DRT Act has been declared as constitutionally valid by the Supreme Court in the case of Union of India v. Delhi High Court Bar Association[16] and the Tribunals established under the DRT Act become fully functional. The certain gaps in the DRT Act have also been filled up by further amendment to the Act. As a consequence to the establishment of Tribunals, the cases pending before the civil courts above Rs.10 lakhs and Decreed cases above Rs.10 lakhs had transferred to DRT's.

An analysis of the amount of dues recovered through DRT, revealed that the entire process of recovery of overdue loans through DRTs doesn't show much progress inspite of the functioning of the the full fledged Debt Recovery Tribunals. One of the reason for such slow progress in recovery is the pocedural delay in DRT in disposing off cases and lack of required powers and skill on the part of the Banks/Financial Institutions to enforce the securities without approaching the Courts.

I (C). THE ENACTMENT OF THE SECURITISATION AND RECONSTURCTION OF FINANCIAL ASSETS AND ENFORCEMENT OF SECURITY INTEREST ACT, 2002- SARFAESI STAGE

As discussed above, the Narasimham Committee I and II and Andhyarujna Committee constituted by the Central Government for the purpose of examining banking sector reforms have considered the need for changes in the legal system in respect of these areas. These Committees, inter alia, have suggested enactment of a new legislation for securitisation and empowering banks and financial institutions to take possession of the securities and sell them without the intervention of the Court. Acting on these suggestions, the Securitisation and Reconstruction of Financial Assets and Enforcement of Security Interest Ordinance, 2002 was promulgated by the Central Government on 21st June 2002 to regulate securitisation and reconstruction of financial assets and enforcement of security interest and for matters connected

[16] Union of India v. Delhi High Court Bar Association, AIR 2002 SC 1479

therewith or incidental thereto. The ordinance got the assent of the President and became an Act. The Act in effect will enable the banks and financial institutions to realize long- term assets, manage problem of liquidity, asset liability mismatches and improve recovery by exercising powers to take possession of securities, sell them and reduce nonperforming assets by adopting measures for recovery or reconstruction.

The Government of India accepted the recommendations of the Narasimham and

Andhyarujina Committees and that led to enactment of the Securitisation and Reconsturction of Financial Assets and Enforcement of Security Interest Act, 2002 (for short 'the SARFAESI Act'), which can be termed as one of the most radical legislative measures taken by the Parliament for ensuring that dues of secured creditors including banks, financial institutions are recovered from the defaulting borrowers without any obstruction. For the first time, the secured creditors have been empowered to take steps for recovery of their dues without intervention of the courts or tribunals.

However, effective implementation of the SARFAESI Act was delayed by more than two years because several writ petitions were filed in the High Courts and the Supreme Court questioning the vires of the Act. The matter was finally decided by the Hon'ble Supreme Court in Mardia Chemicals v. Union of India[17] and the validity of the SARFAESI Act was upheld except the condition of

deposit of 75% amount enshrined in section 17(2). The Court referred to the recommendations of the Narasimham and Andhyarujina Committees on the issue of constitution of special tribunals to deal with cases relating to recovery of the dues of banks, etc and observed that one of the measures recommended in the circumstances was to vest the financial institutions through special statues, the power of sale of the assets without intervention of the court and for reconstruction of assets. It is thus to be seen that the question of non-recoverable or delayed recovery of debts advanced by the Banks was considered in depth by the Committees specially constituted consisting of the experts in the field. In the prevalent situation where the amounts of dues are huge and hope of early recovery is less, it cannot be said that a more effective legislation for the purpose was uncalled for or that it could not be resorted to. It is again to be noted that after the Report of the Narasimham Committee, yet another Committee was constituted headed by Mr.Andhyarujina for bringing about the needed steps within the legal

framework. While upholding the constitutionality of the SARFAESI Act, the Hon'ble Supreme Court was unable to find much substance in the submission made on behalf of the petitioners that while the Recovery of Debts Due to Banks and Financial Institutions Act was in operation it was uncalled for to have yet another legislation for the recovery of the mounting dues like the SARFAESI Act. Considering the totality of circumstances and the financial climate world over, if it was thought as a matter of policy to have yet speedier legal method to recover the dues, such a policy decision cannot be faulted with nor is it a matter to be gone into by the courts to test

the legitimacy of such a measure relating to financial policy.

On examination of various judgements of Supreme Court on various provisions of the SARFAESI Act, it is oberved that on large number of occassions, the spirit and intention of the Parliament in enacting SARFAESI Act was uplouded by the Hon'ble Supreme Court of India. In its judgement in United Bank of India v Satyawat Tondon and others[18] Hon'ble Supreme Court observed that with a view to give impetus to the industrial development of the country, the Central and State Governments encouraged the banks and other financial institutions to formulate liberal policies for grant of loan and other financial facilities to those who wanted to set up new industrial units or expand the existing units. Many hundred thousand took advantage of easy financing by the banks and other financial institutions but a large number of them did not repay the amount of loan. Not only this, they instituted frivolous cases and succeeded in persuading the Civil Courts to pass orders of injunction against the steps taken by banks and financial institutions to recover their dues. Due to lack of adequate infrastructure and non- availability of manpower, the regular courts could not accomplish the task of expeditiously adjudicating the cases instituted by banks and other financial institutions for recovery of their dues. As a result, several hundred crores of public money got blocked in unproductive ventures.

II. CHALLENGES FACED BY THE RECOVERY OF DEBTS DUE TO BANKS AND FINANCIAL INSTITUTIONS ACT, 1993

For few years, the new dispensation under the recovery of debts due to banks and financial institutions act, 1993 worked well and the officers appointed to man the Tribunals worked with great zeal for ensuring that cases involving recovery of the dues of banks and financial

institutions are decided expeditiously. However, with the passage of time, the proceedings before the Tribunals became synonymous with those of the regular courts and the lawyers representing the borrowers and defaulters used every possible mechanism and dilatory tactics to impede the expeditious adjudication of such cases.

The survey conducted by the Ministry of Finance, Government of India revealed that as in 2001, a sum of more than Rs.1,20,000/- crores was due to the banks and financial institutions and this was adversely affecting the economy of the country. Therefore, the Government of India asked the Narasimham Committee to suggest measures for expediting the recovery of debts due to banks and financial institutions. In its Second Report, the Narasimham Committee noted that the nonperforming assets of most of the public sector banks were abnormally high and the existing mechanism for recovery of the same was wholly insufficient. In Chapter VIII of the report, the Committee noted that the evaluation of legal framework has not kept pace with the changing commercial practice and financial sector reforms and as a result of that the economy could not reap full benefits of the reform process. The Committee made various suggestions for bringing about radical changes in the existing adjudication mechanism.

The Committee suggested that the existing laws should be changed not only for facilitating speedy recovery of the dues of banks, etc but also for quick resolution of disputes arising out of the action taken for recovery of such dues. The Andhyarujina Committee constituted by the Central Government for examining banking sector reforms also considered the need for changes in the legal system. Both, the Narasimham and Andhyarujina Committees suggested enactment of new legislation for securitization and empowering the banks and financial institutions to take possession of the securities and sell them without intervention of the court.

The studys shows that as far as India is concerned, the legal impediments and time consuming nature of asset disposal process is throwing lot of challenges for Bankers in resolving the issues pertaining to NPA's. It is also observed that in countries like China, Thailand, Korea, Japan also time consuming, expensive and complicated legal systems are impediments in resolving the issues of NPA's[19].In the Financial Stability Report[20] by the Reserve Bank of India, it is stated that effectiveness of various measures to improve the asset quality of banks will also depend on

[19] 14A comparative study of Non Performing Assets in India in the Global context- similarities and dissimilarities, remedial measures- paper by Shri.Prashanth K Reddy, The Indian Institute of Management Ahmedabad, India.

the efficient functioning of the Debt Recovery Tribunals (DRTs). The shortcomings and loopholes of the Recovery of Debts Due to Banks and Financial Institutions Act have paved the way for introduction of the Securitisation and Revonstruction of Assets and Enforcement of Security Interest Act in 2002.

III.   THE BACKLOG OF PENDING CASES IN DEBT RECOVERY TRIBUNALS

The backlog of pending cases in Debt Recovery Tribunals (DRT) have doubted in recent past. As per the data from the Department of Financial Services, Govt. of India. 59,645 cases involving

`3.74 trillion of bank loans were pending before DRTs, at end of December,2014 compared to 47,933 cases involving 1.78 trillion of loans ar the end of December, 2013[21]. Hence, it is observed that given the large amount of bad loans on the books of banks, and the pressure on banks to resolve stressed assets, the numbers of pending cases increased. These statistics shows that while the government and the banking regulator are moving towards stronger debt recovery rules, including a proposed new bankruptcy law, the process of actual loan recovery remains at slow pace.

In this context, the introduction of the bankruptcy law will give a lot of power to the lenders when dealing with non-performing assets of borrowers. Though under the scheme of DRT Act, the Tribunals are supposed to dispose of a matter referred to it within 180 days of the receipt of an application, the study found that in rarest of rare case only the Tribunals were able to deliver orderwithin the stipulated time.

As of now, there are currently 33 such tribunals. According to the four years of data available, in 2011, these courts had 54,061 cases pending before them, which involved `1.46 trillion in loans. The number of cases and the amount fell in 2012, only to rise over the next two years— hitting a fouryear high in 2014. On an average, the DRTs have been clearing 11,000 to 12,000 cases a year. This means that even if there is no further build-up of cases, it would take more than five years to clear the current backlog.

The rapid addition of bad loans over the last three years and failures of big corporate debt restructuring exercises have led to an increase in the number of cases being referred to the DRTs. At 39 listed banks, gross nonperforming assets (NPAs) rose 27.69% to `3.21 trillion in the

---

[21] www.livemint.com(accessed on 28/10/2015)

June,2015 quarter from `2.51 trillion in the yearago quarter. Overall stressed assets, which include restructured assets, rose to 11.1% of total advances as of March, compared with 10.7% in September 2014, according to the Reserve Bank of India (RBI). The Table depicting the backlog of pending cases in DRT is given below[22]:-

The multiple administrative issues faced by the Tribunals is one of the reasons for slow bad loan resolution. There are a number of DRTs where presiding officers have retired, but new ones are yet to be appointed. At some places, the load of pending cases is so high, the tribunals are not able to cope with the pressure," said the banker. In his budget speech in July 2014, finance minister Arun Jaitley said six new DRTs would be set up in Chandigarh, Bengaluru, Ernakulum, Dehradun, Siliguri and Hyderabad. However, these Tribunals are yet to commence functioning. In this research, it is found that repeated appeals that every case goes through is another reason for slow resolution. The best way to see quick movement, Luthra said, would be to set a ceiling on appeals, depending on the amount of money involved in each case. It is also required to bring more transparency and accountability in the way the cases in Tribunals are being dealt with. The introduction of Bankruptcy Code is another solution to expedite the resolution of bad accounts.

IV.   THE CHALLENGES SUBSEQUENT TO THE ENACTMENT OF THE SECURITISATION AND RECONSTURCTION OF FINANCIAL ASSETS AND ENFORCEMENT OF SECURITY INTEREST ACT, 2002

In the course of development of recovery laws pertaining to Banks, the SARFAESI Act gain more importance and acceptance. However, It also faces a number of challenges from different quarters primarily on the following grounds:-

1.   Arbitrary powers to Banks

The main contention of the those who are challenging the vires of certain provisions of the Act is that the banks and the financial institutions have been vested with arbitrary powers, without any guidelines for its exercise and also without providing any appropriate and adequate mechanism to decide the disputes relating to the correctness of the demand, its validity and the actual amount

²² www.livemint.com (accessed on 28/10/2015)

of dues, sought to be recovered from the borrowers. The offending provisions as contained under the Act, are such that, it all has been made one sided affair while enforcing drastic measures of sale of the property or taking over the management or the possession of the secured assets without affording any opportunity to the borrower.

In fact, the contention of the critics of SARFAESI is that there was no occasion to enact such a draconian legislation to find a short-cut to realize the dues without their ascertainment but which the secured creditor considered to be the dues and declare the same as non-performing assets (NPAs).

Out of the total NPAs which are considered to be about one lakh crores, about half of it is due against priority sector like agriculture, etc. The dues between 10 lakhs to one crore constitute only 13.90 per cent of the total dues. Further, it is submitted, that there is already a special enactment providing for recovery of dues of banks and financial institutions. Therefore, it was not necessary to enact yet another legislation containing drastic steps and procedure depriving the debtors of any fair opportunity to defend themselves from the onslaught of the harsh steps as provided under the Act.

2. No provisions for Lenders Liability

Another criticism against the Sarfaesi Act was that no provision has been made to take into account the lenders liability, though at one time it was considered necessary to have an enactment relating to lenders liability and a bill was also intended to be introduced, as it was considered that it is necessary for the lenders as well to conduct themselves responsibly towards the borrowers. It is submitted that despite such a statement, as indicated above, on the floor of the House, neither any such law has been enacted so far nor any care has been taken to introduce such safeguards in the Act to protect the borrowers against their vulnerability to arbitrary or irresponsible action on the part of the lenders. On a comparative basis, in relation to other countries, it is submitted that the percentage of NPA of as against the GDP is only 6 per cent in India which is much less as compared to China, Malaysia, Thailand, Japan, South Korea and other countries. Therefore, it is evident that the resort has been taken to a drastic legislation, under misapprehension that other ways and means have failed to recover the dues from the borrowers.

3. Non-adjudicatory and Non-judicial

The judicial proceedings without the intervention of the Court is an issue which has been vehemently opposed by the persons who are advocating against the provisions of the Sarfaesi Act. Their contention is that a security interest can be enforced by the secured creditor straightaway without intervention of the court just on default in repayment of an instalment and non-compliance of a notice of 60 days in that regard, declaring the loan as non-performing asset. Under sub-section 4 of section 13 the secured creditor is entitled to take possession of the secured assets and may transfer the same by way of lease, assignment or sale as provided under clause (a) or under clause (b) to take over the management of the secured assets including the right to transfer any secured assets or to appoint any person as provided in clause (c) to manage the secured assets taken over by the creditor.

Under clause (d) by means of a notice any person who has acquired any of the secured assets from the borrower or who has to pay to the borrower any amount which may cover the secured debt, can be asked to pay it to the secured creditor. All that is provided is that if all the dues with costs and charges and expenses incurred by the creditor are tendered before the date fixed for sale of the assets no further steps shall be taken for sale of the property.

It is submitted that the mechanism provided for recovery of the debt under section 13 does not provide for any adjudicatory forum to resolve any dispute which may arise in relation to the liability of the borrower to be treated as a defaulter or to see as to whether there has been any violation or lapse on the part of the creditor or in regard to the correctness of the amount sought to be recovered and the interest levied thereupon. On the other hand, section 34 bars the jurisdiction of the Civil court to entertain any suit in respect of any matter which a Debt Recovery Tribunal or the appellate Tribunal is empowered to determine. It also provides that no injunction shall be granted by any court or other authority in respect of any action taken or to be taken in pursuance of any power conferred by or under Act or under the Recovery of Debts due to Banks and Financial Institutions Act, 1993.

Section 35 gives an overriding effect to the provisions of the Act over the provisions contained under any other law. So in effect, before any action is taken under section 13, there is no forum or adjudicatory mechanism to resolve any dispute which may arise in respect of the alleged dues or the NPA.

Appeal provision is only illusory

Many critics of the Sarfaesi Act is of the view that the provision of appeal as contained in

section 17 of the Act is also illusory since an appeal may be preferred within the specified time from the date on which measures under sub-section 4 of section 13 have been taken. The appeal would be maintainable after the possession of the property or the management of the secured assets has been taken over or the property has been sold. Further, an appeal is not entertainable unless 75 per cent of the amount claimed in the notice is deposited by the borrower with the Debt Recovery Tribunal. It would be a matter in the discretion of the Debt Recovery Tribunal to waive the condition of pre deposit or to reduce the amount, for reasons to be recorded therefore. It is submitted that a remedy which is available, after the damage is done and on fulfilment of such an onerous condition as deposit of 75 per cent of the demand, is illusory and a mere farce. It is no real remedy available to a borrower before he is subjected to harsh steps as provided under sub- section (4) of section 13. It is further submitted that after the possession of the secured assets or its management has been taken over by the secured creditor or the property is leased out or sold to any other person, it would not be possible to raise and deposit 75 per cent of the amount claimed by the secured creditor. It is also submitted that once the secured assets are taken over there is hardly any occasion for deposit of 75 per cent of the claim since it is already secured and the management and the possession of the secured assets moves into the hands of the creditor. The position thus is that the borrower is gagged into a helpless position where he cannot ventilate his grievance against the drastic steps taken against him. The doors of the civil court are closed for him and no adjudicatory mechanism is provided before steps are taken under sub-section (4) of section 13. Such a law, it is submitted, isarbitrary and suffers from the vice of unreasonableness.

In so far it relates to section 19 of the Act which provides, in case it is found that possession of the secured assets was wrongfully taken by the secured creditor he may be directed to return the secured assets to the borrower who may also be entitled to such compensation as may be determined by the debt recovery Tribunal or the appellate Tribunal, it is submitted that it is hardly a consolation after harsh steps as provided under sub-section 4 of section 13 have been taken.

The contentions against Section 17 of the SARFAESI Act was considerered positively by the Hon'ble Supreme Court in Mardia Chemicals18 case and strike down the same by declaring it as unconstitutional and against the principles of natural justice.

5. Non-availability of adjudicatory forum

The critics of Sarfaesi Act are of the view that for exercise of power under section 13, certain enquiries would be necessary as to whether a person to whom notice is given is under a liability to pay as also the question of extent of the liability, etc. Further the questions pertaining to law of limitation and bar under consortium agreements, claim of set off/counter claim, creditor's defaults as bailee or its failure to disburse the credit in time, the changeability of penal interest or compound interest or non-appropriation of amount already paid and so on and so forth, all these questions need to be decided. Further the bar of section 22 of the Sick Industrial Companies Act (hereinafter referred to as SICA) also need to be considered. However, there is no adjudicatory body provided under the SARFAESI Act for dealing with such disputes or adjudication of such disputes.

The power which is exercised by the Authorised Officer to enforce security by way of sale, etc. without any determination of disputed questions, under section 13 of the Act, is unconstitutional. The SARFAESI has vested the Authorised Officer to exercise the power without any determination of disputed questions excluding the judicial remedies renders the Act procedurally and substantively unfair, unreasonable and arbitrary. The power of judicial determination is manifestation of sovereign power to determine the legal rights which cannot be vested in private bodies as foreign banks, cooperative banks or non-banking financial institutions etc.

The critics pointed out that the scope of section 13 of the Act is fundamentally different from the scope of power under section 69 of the Transfer of Property Act.The power under section 69 of the Transfer of Property Act is hedged with various restrictions to prevent abuse of power including mortgagors right to have recourse to court both before and after the sale.19 Further, even in case of the English mortgage, it is in the nature of conveyance or absolute transfer of mortgage property with provision of retransfer upon discharge of mortgage. While adequate restrictions were provided under the Transfer of Property Act to protect the interest of the rightful owners of the property, the same care and caution is not provided under the SARFAESI Act.

The scope of section 13 of the Act is fundamentally different from the scope of power under section 69 of the Transfer of Property Act. In terms of 2(f) of the SARFAESI Act, the definition of the word borrower covers even the guarantor. Section 135 of the Contract Act dealt with instances where a guarantor is discharged of his obligation. In view of the bar of section 34 to file a suit in the Civil Court, it is not possible for a guarantor to approach the court to show and establish that he is a discharged guarantor.[23]

Another lacuna is that the word security has not been defined under section 2 of the Act. It is submitted that the Act not to apply to the legal liens. It is submitted that if property is subject to several charge as first charge, second charge and third charge and so on property in relation to only one of them would be NPA and not in relation to other creditors having charge over the property. It is submitted that it is not clear in such a situation how the Act will be workable. Another instance is section 44 of the Transfer of Property Act which deals with the case of transfer by one co-owner and the difficulty to work out the provisions of the Act in such cases.

However, the Banks are defending the allegations by stating that the financial institutions are badly effected by non-recovery of dues and despite the existing laws like, the Recovery of Debts due to Banks and Financial Institutions Act, much could not be achieved, hence it was necessary to take further legislative steps to accelerate recovery of the heavy amount of dues. They contended that after availing the facility of financial assistance quite often the borrowers hardly show interest in repayment of loan which keep on accumulating as a result of which it becomes difficult for the financial institutions to continue the financial assistance to deserving parties due to heavy blockade of money stuck up with the erring borrowers. It is not good for a financial institution to have heavy NPA. They further indicated that since after enforcement of the Act there has been marked improvement in the recovery and quite substantial amount has since been recovered.

The Banks further content that the Act was enacted to curb the menace of growing nonperforming assets (NPAs). It affects the banks and financial institutions which is ultimately against the public interest. Due to non-recovery of the dues, the banks also run out of the financial resources to further carry on the financial activity and to meet the need and requirement of its other depositors and clients. After coming into force of the Recovery of Debts due to Banks and Financial Institutions Act and establishment of Debt Recovery Tribunals the success in

[23] Bank of Maharashtra Ltd v. Official Liquidator, High Court Buildings AIR 1969 Mys. 280. 35

recovery has not been very encouraging. Therefore, need was felt for a faster procedure empowering the secured creditors to recover their dues and for securitisation of financial assets so as to generate maximum monetary liquidity. It has been felt that after coming into force of the Act there is a marked difference in realization of dues and more borrowers are coming forward to pay up the defaulted amount and clear the dues.

The Bankers further highlight that in case a defaulter wants to raise any objection it may be raised in reply to the notice which would obviously be considered by the secured creditor before it would further proceed to take recourse to sub-section 4 of section 13 of the Act. It is further submitted that there will be ample time for a borrower to approach the Debt Recovery Tribunal to seek relief before sale of the secured assets. The remedy as provided under section 17 of the Act is adequate. The bar of jurisdiction of the Civil Court was thought to be necessary to avoid lengthy legal process in realizing the amount due. It is further stated that normally there should be a presumption in favour of validity of legislation more so in regard to the laws relating to economic and financial matters and a few instances here and there of any harsh results would not be a valid consideration to invalidate the law.

V.   RECENT DEVELOPMENT IN SARFAESI/ DRT ACT

As a consequence of the judgement of the Hon'ble Supreme Court in Mardia Chemicals case, the SARFAESI Act was amended by the Union of India. The condition for pre-deposit of 75 per cent of the amount claimed in the notice was removed and the borrowers and guarantors have got right to file appeal before the DRT without deposit of any amount.

The Enforcement of Security Interest and Recovery of Debts Laws (Amendment) Bill, 2011 has been passed by both the Houses of the Parliament i.e. Lok Sabha and Raja Sabha. The Bill also got assent of the President of India on the 3rd January, 2013 and become an Act (Act No.1 of 2013). This Act amended the provisions of the Securitisation and Reconstruction of Financial Assets and Enforcement of Security Interest Act, 2002 and the Recovery of Debts Due to Banks and Financial Institutions Act, 1993. The important highlights of the Amendment Act are as follows:-

BEFORE THE AMENDMENT OF

SARFAESI ACT

AFTER THE AMENDMENT OF

SARFAESI ACT

The banks and financial institutions were required to consider representations from borrowers and communicate their response

within a period of seven (7) days.

The period within which the response is to be sent to the representation of the borrower is enhanced from seven (7) days to fifteen (15) days- [Section 13(3A)].

The banks were not empowered to participate in the bid for purchase of any immovable property in realisation of the claim against the defaulted borrower in situations where banks were unable to find a suitable buyer for such

assets.

Where the sale of immovable property has been postponed for want of a bid of an amount not less than the Reserve Price, any officer of the Bank may bid on behalf of the Bank- [Section 13(5A)(5B)(5C)].

There was no provision for filing caveat against Sarfaesi Application/Appeal.

The Secured Creditor (Bank) or any person may lodge a caveat in anticipation of the Sarfaesi Application/Appeal by the

borrower/guarantor-[Section 18©].

There was no provision to file an affidavit along with the application under Section 14 of the Act for taking physical possession.

The application filed by the Bank under Section 14 of the Act for taking physical possession shall be accompanied by an affidavit duly affirmed by the authorized officer declaring the aggregate amount of dues, confirmation regarding the service of 13(2) notice on the borrower, disposal of objection raised by the borrower, etc –

[Section 14(1)].

In case of financing of a financial asset by more than one secured creditors or joint financing of a financial asset, creditors representing three-fourth in value must agree for exercising the rights conferred

under Section 13(4) of the Act.

In case of financing of a financial asset by more than one secured creditors or joint financing of a financial asset, creditors representing sixty per cent in value must agree for exercising the rights conferred

under Section 13(4) of the Act-[Section

13(9)].

There was no provision empowering the District Mgistrte or the Chief Metropolitan Magistrate to authorize any officer subordinate to him to take possession of the assets and documents under Section 14 of the Act.

The newly inserted Section 14(1A) of the Act, empowers the District Mgistrte or the Chief Metropolitan Magistrate to authorize any officer subordinate to him to take possession of the assets and documents under Section 14 of the Act [Section

14(1A)].

There was no provision to enable the Securitisation and Reconstruction Company to file application for the purpose of substitution of its name in any pending suit, appeal or other proceedings.

The Securitisation and Reconstruction Company may file application before the DRT or Appellate Tribunal for the purpose of substitution of its name in any pending suit, appeal or other proceedings [Section 5(5)].

The Securitisation and Reconstruction of Financial Assets and Enforcement of Security Interest Act, 2002 did not allow

securitisation or reconstruction companies to convert the debt of the borrower

company into equity.

The Amendment Act provide for conversion of any part of debt into shares of a borrower company - [Section 9 (g)].

The multi-state co-operative banks are not included in the definition of banks.

The multi-state co-operative banks are included in the definition of banks –

[Section 2 c (iv)(a)].

There was no provision for registration of transactions of securitisation, reconstruction or creation of security interest in the Central Registry, which are subsisting on or before the establishment of Central Registry or to extend the time for filing of such transaction with the Central Registry.

The provision made for registration of transactions of securitisation, reconstruction or creation of security interest in the Central Registry, which are subsisting on or before the establishment of Central Registry. It also gave powers to the central government to extend the time for filing of such transaction with the

Central Registry - [Section 26 A (1)].

There was no provision wheren the central government may exempt a class or classes of banks or financial institutions from the provisions of this Act on grounds of public

interest.

The central government may exempt a class or classes of banks or financial institutions from the provisions of this Act on grounds of public interest-[Section 31 (A)].

BEFORE THE AMENDMENT OF DRT

ACT

AFTER THE AMENDMENT OF DRT

ACT

There was provision which entitle Bank to file application for refund of the fees paid to DRT if the Bank got settled the account at any stage of the proceedings before the final order is

passed.

The Banks can file application for refund of the fees paid to DRT if the application got settled at any stage of the proceedings before the final order is passed-[Section 19(3A) of the Act].

There was no provision wherein the defendant/borrower were bound to file written statement within the stipulated period of time.

The defendant/borrower shall file written statement within a period of thirty days from the date of service of summons. If the defendant fails to file written statement within the said period, the Presiding Officer may in exceptional cases allow not more than two extensions to the defendant to file written

statement [Section 19(5)].

There was no provision wherein the hearing of the application shall be completed within the stipulated period of time.

The hearing of the application shall be continued from day-to-day and no adjournment shall be granted more than three times to a party and where there are three or more parties, the total number of adjournments shall not

exceed six[Section 19(5A)].

There was no provision wherein the Presiding Officer can impose cost for granting

adjournment.

The Presiding Officer has been empowered to impose cost for grant adjournments- [Section

19(5A)].

The multi-State co-operative banks were not

The multi-State co-operative banks have been

included in the definition of bank in the

Recovery of Debts Due to Banks and Financial Institutions Act, 1993.

included in the definition of bank in the

Recovery of Debts Due to Banks and Financial Institutions Act, 1993[Section 2(d) (vi)].

There was no provision enabling the Debts Recovery Tribunal empowered to pass an order acknowledging settlement or compromise between Bank and borrower/guarantor.

In case of settlement or compromise between the Bank and the borrower, the Debts Recovery Tribunal is empowered to pass an order acknowledging any such settlement or

compromise [Section 19(20A)].

After the amendments in SARFAESI & DRT Act, the Government and Regulators such as RBI are working on various measures to improve the enforcement of the provisions of the recovery laws. Recently, the Reserve Bank, on January 30, 2014, has issued a 'Framework to Revitalise the Distressed Assets in the Economy', wherein banks would recognise at an early stage the stress in their assets and take prompt steps towards resolution/ recovery of distressed assets and detailed guidelines in this regard were issued on February 26, 2014. The framework has identified certain structural impediments in the way of smooth resolution/ recovery of stressed assets of banks and suggested steps, such as, revamping the SARFAESI Act, revitalizing DRTs, etc. and rejuvenating Asset Reconstruction Companies, are also being mooted.

CHAPTER – 4 CONSTITUTIONAL AND REGULATORY FRAMEWORK OF

RECOVERY LAWS RELATING TO BANKS AND FINANCIAL INSTITUTIONS

" Bad laws are the worst form of tyranny "

Edmund Burke (1729-1797) British political writer

It is generally believed that the processes involved in a suit filed for recovery of debts before a civil court are proverbially disconcerting to the Banks/Financial Institutions in recovering the huge backlog of Non-Performing Assets. Very often, therefore, the protracted delay in recovering debt will result in a loss to the Banks/Financial Institutions in real terms, as the time spent for the process itself would have substantially eroded the value of money, even if recovered fully. The delay in litigation has equally affected the party on the other side i.e. borrowers and guarantors, exposing them to costly and time consuming legal battle. With the objective, therefore, of providing banks and financial institutions with a speedier and more efficient mode of recovery of debts, the legislature has provided for the establishment of special courts by enacting the Recovery of Debts Due to Banks and Financial Institutions Act, 1993. The Recovery of Debts Due to Banks and Financial Institutions Act, 1993 (hereafter referred to as DRT Act) was enacted by the Parliament as the Act no.51 of 1993.

I. The Constitutionality of the provisions of the Recovery of Debts Due to Banks and Financial Institutions Act, 1993

A number of writ petitions were filed in different High Courts in India challenging the constitutionality of the Recovery of Debts Due to Banks and Financial Institutions Act, 1993. On analysis of the judgement of various High Courts, the legal issues highlighted by different High Courts are summarised as follows:

The Delhi High Court Judgement

The validity of the DRT Act was first challenged before the Delhi High Court. By its decision reported in Delhi High Court Bar Association and another v. Union of India and others[24], the High Court held that though Tribunal could be constituted by Parliament even though it was not within the purview of Arts.323-A and 323-B of the Constitution and that the expression "administration of justice" as appearing in Entry 11-A of List III of the Seventh Schedule to the Constitution would include Tribunals as well administering justice; the DRT Act was unconstitutional as it erodes the independence of the judiciary and was irrational, discriminatory, unreasonable, arbitrary and was hit by Art.14 of the Constitution..

The reasonig given by the High Court while delaring the Recovery of Debts Due to Banks and Financial Institutions Act, 1993 as irrational and arbitrary was that Section 17 of the Act did not have a provision for a counter-claim as provided under the provisions of the Code of Civil Procedure . The Act also lowered the authority of the High Court vis-a-vis the Tribunal in view of the fact that suits for recovery of money exceeding Rs.10 lacs are to be filed before the Tribunal while the suits for an amount between Rs.5 lacs and Rs.10 lacs was to be filed before the Delhi High Court and for less than Rs.5 lacs before the subordinate Courts. This lowered the status of the High Court in as much as the Tribunal, which was presided by an officer who did not have the status of a High Court Judge, would be deciding the suits for recovery of money exceeding Rs.10 lacs.

Another criticism against the Act was that it eroded the independence of the judiciary since the jurisdiction of Civil Courts had been truncated and vested in the Tribunal. It also came to the conclusion that the independence of the judiciary was eroded as the High Court had no role to play in the appointment of the Presiding Officers.

2. The Guwahati High Court Judgment

The Guwahati High Court also considered the validity of the DRT Act. By judgement in Assam Leather Industry vs Union Of India (Uoi) And Ors[25], the High Court came to the conclusion that though the Parliament has legislative competence to enact the law, but as it had abrogated

/negated the power of judicial review, the Act was void as it had violated the basic feature of the

[24] Delhi High Court Bar Association and another v. Union of India and others reported in AIR 1995 Delhi 323.

[25] 23Gauhati High Court-Assam Leather Industry vs Union of India (UOI) And Ors. on 16 August, 1999: 2001 104 CompCas 115 Gauhati/Indian Kanoon - http://indiankanoon.org/doc/1237648/

Constitution. It further held that Section 17 need to be stuck down as it gives jurisdiction, powers and authority which are unreasonable. It also struck down the appointment of Recovery Officer and held the modes for recovery of debts under Section 25 and 28(1) and (2) as being arbitrary, unreasonable and without any guidelines, control, etc. It further quashed Section 31 which deals with the transfer of suits/proceedings and Section 34(1) which gives overriding effect to the Act.

3. Karnataka High Court Judgement

While considering the validity of the DRT Act, the Karnataka High Court in the case of D.K.Abdul Khader and others v. Union of India and others[26] came to the conclusion that the Parliament did not have the legislative competence to enact the Act in as much as Entry 11-A of List III could not include "Tribunal" and furthermore that the Parliament could not exercise power to enact this law under the provisions of Art.323-A or 323-B of the constitution. In other words, a Tribunal could not be constituted for any matter not specified in Art.323-A and 323-B.

4. The Supreme Court of India Judgement

All the aforesaid decisions of the High Court were challenged before the Hon'ble Supreme Court of India in Union of India and another v. Delhi High Court Bar Association and others[27]. The main contention of the critics of the DRT Act was that the Act is unreasonable and are violative of Art.14 of the Constitution and that the same is beyond the legislative competence of the Parliament.

The Hon'ble Supreme Court while analyzing the orders of the High Court given the following observations:-

I. The power of Parliament to enact a law, which is not covered by an Entry, List II and List

III, is absolute.

II. While Arts.323-A and 323-B specifically enable the legislatures to enact laws for the establishment of Tribunals, in relation to the matters specified therein, the power of the

[26] K.Abdul Khader and others v. Union of India and others reported in AIR 2001 Kant 179

[27] Union of India and another v. Delhi High Court Bar Association and others reported in AIR 2002 SC 1479, 2002(2) SCR 450, 2002 (4) SCC 275.

Parliament to enact a law constituting a Tribunal, like the Banking Tribunal, which is not covered by any of the matters specified in Art 323-A or 323-B, is not taken away.

III. Articles 323-A and 323-B are enabling provisions which specifically enable the setting up of Tribunals contemplated by the said Articles. These Articles, however, cannot be interpreted to mean that it prohibits the legislature from establishing Tribunals not covered by these Articles, as long as there is legislative competence under an appropriate entry in the Seventh Schedule. Articles 323-A and 323-B do not take away that legislative competence. The contrary view expressed by the Karnataka High Court in D.K.Abdula Khadder's case[28] does not lay down the correct law and the Ld. Supreme Court expressly disapproves of the same.

IV. Entry 45 of List I relates to "Banking". Banking operations would, inter alia, include accepting of loans and deposits, granting of loans and recovery of the debts due to the bank. The recovery of dues is an essential function of any banking institution. In exercise of its legislative power relating to banking, the parliament can provide the mechanism by which monies due to the Banks and Financial Institutions can be recovered. The Tribunals have been set up in regard to the debts due to the banks. The special machinery of a Tribunal which has been constituted as per the preamble of the Act "for expeditious adjudication and recovery of debts due to banks and financial institutions and for matters connected therewith or incidental thereto" would squarely fall within the ambit of Entry 45 of List I. Setting up of an adjudicatory body like the Banking Tribunal relating to transactions in which banks and financial institutions are concerned would clearly fall under Entry 45 of List I giving the Parliament specific power to legislate in relation thereto.

V. The Supreme Court is unable to agree with the decision of the Delhi High Court that the DRT Act or any other provision thereof is in any way arbitrary or bad in law. During the pendency of these appeals, the DRT Act has been amended and whatever lacunae's or infirmities existed have now been removed by the said Amending Act and with the framing of more rules. For example: Rules have been framed in 1998 for the appointing of Presiding Officers of the Tribunals as well as the Presiding Officers of the Appellate Tribunals. The Rules contemplate appointments being made by a Selection Committee. Each of the Selection Committee is to consist of the Chief

[28] D.K.Abdul Khader and others v. Union of India and others reported in AIR 2001 Kant 179 44

Justice of India or a Judge of the Supreme Court as nominated by the Chief Justice of India along with other members referred to in the said Rules. The Selection Committee so constituted would ensure fair and impartial selection of competent persons to act as Presiding Officers of the Tribunal.

VI. There is no absolute right in anyone to demand that his dispute is to be adjudicated upon only by a Civil Court. It is by reason of the provisions of the Code of Civil Procedure that the Civil Courts had the right, prior to the enactment of the Debt Recovery Act, to decide the suits for recovery filed by the banks and financial institutions. This forum, namely, that of a Civil Court, now stands replaced by a Banking Tribunal in respect of the debts due to the bank. When in the Constitution Arts.323-A and 323-B contemplate establishment of a Tribunal and that does not erode the independence of the judiciary, there is no reason to presume that the Banking Tribunals and the Appellate Tribunals so constituted would not be independent or that justice would be denied to the defendants or that the independence of the judiciary would stand eroded.

VII. The Tribunals, whether they pertain to Income-tax or Sales Tax or Excise and Customs or Administration, have now become an essential part of the judicial system in this country. Such specialized institutions may not strictly come within the concept of the judiciary, as envisaged by Art.50, but it cannot be presumed that such Tribunals are not an effective part of the justice delivery system, like Courts of law. It will be seen that for a person to be appointed as a Presiding Officer of DRT, he should be one who is qualified to be a District Judge and in case of appointment of the Presiding Officer of the appellate Tribunal he is or has been, qualified to be a judge of a High Court or has been a member of the Indian Legal Service who has held a post in Grade I for at least three years. It has to be borne in mind that the decision of the appellate Tribunal is not final, in the sense that the same can be subjected to judicial review by the High Court under Arts.226 and 227 of the Constitution.

VIII.   With the establishment of the Tribunals, Section 31 provides for the transfer of pending cases from Civil Courts to the Tribunal. The Court does not find such a provision being in any way bad in law. Once a Debt Recovery Tribunal has been established and the jurisdiction of Courts barred by Section 18 of the Act, it would be only logical that any matter pending in the Civil Court should stand transferred to the Tribunal.

IX.   The Guwahati High Court held that Sections 25 and 28 are arbitrary and unreasonable, being without any guidelines or control. These observations were made prior to the amendment of Sections 25 and 28. After amendment, Section 25 provides for modes of recovery of debts either by attachment and sale or arrest or appointment of a Receiver and Section 28 provides for modes of recovery in addition to the ones specified in Section 25. The Hon'ble court held that a perusal of the aforesaid provisions cannot lead one to the conclusion that the same are arbitrary, unreasonable or without any guidelines. It is quite clear that in order to recover the debts, the Recovery Officer has to attach and sell the immovable property and that for protection and preservation of the same, and he has the power to appoint a Receiver for the management thereof.

X.   By virtue of Section 29 of the Act, the provisions of the Second and Third Schedules to the Income Tax Act, 1961 and the Income Tax(Certificate Proceedings) Rules, 1962, has become applicable for the realization of the dues by the Recovery Officer. Detailed procedure for recovery is contained in these schedules to the Income-tax Act, including provisions relating to arrest and detention of the defaulter. It cannot, therefore, be said that the Recovery Officer would act in an arbitrary manner. Furthermore, Section 30, after amendment by the Amendment Act, 2000, gives a right to any person aggrieved by an order of the Recovery Officer, to prefer an appeal to the Tribunal. There is, therefore, sufficient safeguard which has been provided in the event of the Recovery Officer acting in an arbitrary or unreasonable manner. The provisions of Sections 25 and 28 are, therefore, not bad in law.

XI.   The Hon'ble Court while allowing the appeals of the Union of India and the Bank held that the Recovery of Debts Due to Banks and Financial Institutions Act, 1993 is a valid piece of legislation. As a result thereof, the writ petitions or appeals filed by various parties challenging the validity of the said Act or some of the provisions thereof are dismissed.

After declaring the DRT Act as constitutionally valid, the Tribunals as constituted under the Act were become functional and started delivering judgements. In principle, the essential points of difference between a proceeding before the Tribunal and a suit before a Civil Court lie firstly in the procedures required to be followed by each, and secondly in the need of the applicant to establish existence of debt, and thirdly, in the scope for hearing of arguments over technical lapses of the creditor, if any. Since the proceedings before the Debt Recovery Tribunals are

guided by the principles of natural justice and not by the rules under CPC, the proceedings were faster than the civil courts.

As the Recovery of Debts Due to Banks and Financial Institutions Act, 1993 was made in haste; there were certain lacunae which were questioned in various High Courts and also Supreme Court. Therefore the Act was amended widening its scope and giving it more teeth. After passing of the Recovery of Debts Due to Banks and Financial Institutions (Amendment) Act, 2000, the Supreme Court delivered a comprehensive judgement in Civil Appeal No.2536 of 2000, dated 16-04-2000 in Allahabad Bank vs. Canara Bank and another,[29] dealing with almost all important provisions of the Act.

The said case raises issues relating to the impact of the provisions of the Recovery of Debts due to Banks and Financial Institutions Act, 1993 on the provisions of the Companies Act, 1956. The dispute was between two nationalized Banks, the Allahabad Bank on the one hand which has obtained a simple money decree against the debtor-company (M/s.M.S.Shoes (East)

Co. Ltd) from the Debt Recovery Tribunal at Delhi under the RDB Act and the Canara Bank on the other, whose claim as a secured creditor is still pending before the same Tribunal against the same company. The Allahabad Bank appealed before the Supreme Court against an order passed by the learned Company Judge under Sections 442 and 537 of the Companies Act, staying the sale proceedings taken out by the Allahabad Bank before the Recovery Officer under the DRT Act. Applications for winding up the defendant company are pending in the Delhi High Court. The point raised by the respondent-Canara Bank was that the appellant Allahabad Bank is obliged to seek leave of the Company Court under the Companies Act, 1956 and the Company Court can stay these proceedings as aforesaid under Sections 442 and 537 for the ultimate purpose of deciding the priorities, in the event of a winding up order or other order appointing a provisional liquidator being passed under Section 446(1) of the Companies Act, 1956.

The appellant, Allahabad Bank contended that the DRT Act is a special statute intended for expeditious adjudication and recovery of debts due to banks and financial institutions and it contains two crucial provisions. One of them is Section 18 which ousts the jurisdiction of all courts or other authorities (except the Supreme Court and the High Court exercising powers

[29] Allahabad Bank vs. Canara Bank and another, AIR 2000 SC1535, 2000(4) SCC 406

under Articles 226, 227) in relation to matters covered by Section 17 and that Section 17 covers the entire procedure from the filing of an application under Section 19, to the adjudication and recovery. The proceedings under the RDB Act cannot be stayed by the Company Court not can they be transferred to the Company Court. No leave of the Company Court is necessary either for filing of the OA for adjudication of the debt nor for executing the decree passed by the Tribunal. Section 34(2) proceedings saves only six statutes from the purview of Section 34(1). The Companies Act, 1956 is not one of them. Hence, the DRT Act, 1993 overrides Sections 442, 537 and also Section 446 of the Companies Act. It is contended that even otherwise Section 446 cannot be invoked in this case because there is no winding up order nor an order appointing a provisional liquidator so far. Only Section 529-A of the Companies Act is attracted and that too for a limited purpose if a question of "workman's portion" is involved.

As against the arguments of the appellant, the respondent i.e. Canara Bank submitted that when a winding up petition is pending in the Company Court, it is necessary that the leave of the Company Court is obtained for obtaining a decree before the Tribunal or for execution before the Recovery Officer. Leave is necessary under Section 537 even if no winding up order is passed. The Company Court alone can sell the properties of the company in the winding up proceedings. The recovery proceedings must be stayed and then the proceedings must be transferred to the Company Court and thereafter, once the proceeds of sale come before the Company Court, the said Court alone will have to distribute the monies according to priorities as mentioned in Sections 446(2) (d), 529, 529-A and 530.

After hearing both the parties, the Hon'ble Supreme Court drawn the following points for the consideration:-

i. Whether in respect of proceedings under the RDB Act at the stage of adjudication for the money due to the Banks or Financial Institutions and at the stage of execution for recovery or monies under the RDB Act, the Tribunal and the Recovery Officers are conferred exclusive jurisdiction in their respective spheres?
ii. Whether for initiation of various proceedings by the Banks and Financial Institutions under the RDB Act, leave of the Company Court is necessary under Sections 537 before a winding up order is passed against the Company or before provisional liquidator is appointed under Section

446(1) and whether the Company Court can pass orders of stay of proceedings before the Tribunal, in exercise of powers under section 442?

iii. Whether after a winding up order is passed under Section 446(1), the Company Court can stay proceedings under the RDB Act, transfer them to itself and also decide questions of liability, execution and priority under Section 446(2) and (3) read with Sections 529, 529-A and 530 etc., of the Companies Act or whether these questions are all within the exclusive jurisdiction of the Tribunal?

iv. Whether, in case it is decided that the distribution of monies is to be done only by the Tribunal, the provisions of Section 73 CPC and sub-clauses (1) and (2) of Section 529, Section 530 of the Companies Act or whether these questions are all within the exclusive jurisdiction of the Tribunal?

v. Whether in view of provisions in Section 19(2) and 19(19) as introduced by Ordinance 1 of 2000, the Tribunal can permit the appellant Bank alone to appropriate the entire sale proceeds realized by the appellant except to the limited extent restricted by Section 529-A?

Can the secured creditors like the Canara Bank claim under Section 19(19) any part of the realizations made by the Recovery Officer and is there any difference between cases where the secured creditors opts to stand outside the winding up and where he goes before the Company Court?

vi. What is the relief to be granted on the facts of the case since the Recovery Officer has now sold some properties of the company and the monies are lying partly in the Tribunal or partly in this Court?

As regards, point no.1 concerning the question as to the exclusive jurisdiction of the Tribunal and the Recovery Officer in their respective spheres, the Hon'ble Court held as follows :-.

The DRT Act is the result of two reports, one of 1981 of a Committee headed by Sri.T.Tiwari and the other by Sri.M.Narasimhan in 1991. As on 30-09-1990 more than 15 lakh cases filed by public sector Banks and about 304 cases filed by financial institutions were pending in various civil courts and recovery of debts to Banks in a sum of Rs.5622 crores and to financial

institutions in a sum of Rs.391 crores, was held up. That was the immediate cause for the passing of the Act.

The Hon'ble Court held that the jurisdiction of the Tribunal in regard to adjudication is exclusive.

The DRT Act requires the Tribunal alone to decide applications for recovery of debts due to Banks or Financial Institutions. Once the Tribunal passes an order that the debt is due, the Tribunal has to issue a certificate under Section 19(22) to the Recovery Officer for recovery of the debt specified in the certificate. The jurisdiction of the Recovery Officer is exclusive. The certificate granted under Section 19(22) has to be executed only by the Recovery Officer.

Thus, the adjudication of liability and the recovery of the amount by execution of the certificate are respectively within the exclusive jurisdiction of the Tribunal and the Recovery Officer and no other Court or authority much less the Civil Court or the Company Court can go into the said questions relating to the liability and the recovery except as provided in the Act. The Tiwari Committee which recommended the constitution of a Special Tribunal in 1981 for recovery of debts due to Banks and Financial Institutions stated in its Report that the exclusive jurisdiction of the Tribunal must relate not only in regard to the adjudication of the liability but also in regard to the execution proceedings.

As regards the questions whether the Company Court can stay proceedings before the Tribunal or the Recovery Officer under Section 442 and whether the said Court can stall proceedings under Section 537 unless leave is obtained and whether the Company Court alone can distribute and decide priorities among creditors or whether the Tribunal can do this in view of Section

19(19) of the DRT Act, the Hon'ble Court held as follows:-

The Hon'ble Court held that the Company Court has no jurisdiction to entertain and adjudicate the claims of Banks and financial institutions. On the same parity of reasoning, there is no need for the appellant to seek leave of the Company Court to proceed with its claim before the Debt Recovery Tribunal or in respect of the execution proceedings before the Recovery Officer.

Nor can they be transferred to the Company Court. The Hon'ble Court further held that the purpose of DRT Act is something more important than the purpose of sections 442, 446 and 537 of the Companies Act.

The legal complexities relating to the jurisdiction of the DRT to entertain execution petition, when decree of Civil Court is for more than Rs.10.00 lacs came up for consideration before the Hon'ble Supreme Court of India in Punjab National Bank, Dasuya v. Chajju Ram and others[30].

In this case, the appellant filed a suit for recovery of Rs.6, 19,250 in the civil court. By judgment dated 16-02-1994, the trial court decreed the suit for the aforesaid amount with interest. In the meanwhile on 25-6-1993, the Recovery of Debts Due to Banks and Financial Institutions Act, 1993 had come into force. On 18-02-1997 the appellant moved an application before the Civil Court, Dasuya for transfer of the execution proceedings to the DRT, Jaipur. This application was allowed and the trial court ordered the transfer of the execution proceedings to the DRT, Jaipur. The respondents thereupon filed a revision petition in the High Court. By judgement, the High Court came to the conclusion, while reversing the decision of the trial court, that the execution proceedings could not be transferred and it is only the civil court, which had passed the decree, which could execute the same. Against the said High Court order, an appeal by special leave was filed before the Hon'ble Supreme Court.

The Hon'ble court held that Section 31 contemplates not only the transfer of a suit but also transfer of a proceeding which may be other than a suit, like an execution application. As and when the amount due to the Bank under the decree became more than Rs.10 lakhs and an application for execution was filed, it could only be entertained by the DRT and not by the civil court. Hence, the Hon'ble Supreme Court allowed the appeal and the judgement of the High Court was set aside.

II. THE CONSTITUATIONAL VALIDITY OF SARFAESI ACT

The constitutional validity of the SARFAESI Act was considered by the Hon'ble Supreme Court of India in the popular case of Mardia Chemicals - Mardia Chemicals Ltd V Union of India[31].

[30] Punjab National Bank, Dasuya v. Chajju Ram and others, AIR 2000 SC 2671

[31] Punjab National Bank, Dasuya v. Chajju Ram and others, AIR 2000 SC 2671.

The Hon'ble Supreme Court of India upheld the validity of the Act and its provisions except that of sub-section (2) of Section 17 of the Act, which was declared ultra vires of Article 14 of the Constitution of India. It was also observed in Mardia Chemicals case that where a secured creditor has taken action under Section 13(4) of the Act, in such cases it would be open to borrowers / guarantors to file appeals under Section 17 of the Act within the limitation as prescribed.

1. AFTER AFFECTS OF THE DECISION IN MARDIA CHEMICALS –

The Act was amended w.e.f. 11.11.2004 in the light of the observations of the Hon'ble Supreme Court in Mardia Chemicals Case and the following major amendments to the Act were carried out –

- Section 3-A was inserted providing for an opportunity to the borrower to make a representation or raise objections against the demand notice issued under sub-section (2) of Section 13 and disposal of such representation within one week from the date of its receipt. A proviso was inserted that the reasons communicated to the borrower in response to the representation shall not confer any right upon him to prefer an application to the Debt Recovery Tribunal.
- Sub-section (2) of Section 17 which provided that the appeal filed by the Borrower against the measures taken by the secured creditor under sub-section (4) of section 13 shall not be entertained unless the borrower deposited with the Debt Recovery Tribunal 75% of the amount claimed under demand notice with a proviso that the Debts Recovery Tribunal may waive or reduce the amount for reasons to be recorded in writing have been substituted with the provision that the Debt Recovery Tribunal shall consider whether any of the measures referred in sub- section (4) of section 13 taken by the secured creditor are in accordance with the provisions of the Act and rules made there under.
- The provision of Appeal to the Appellate Tribunal under section 18 were also modified accordingly, providing that the appellate tribunal shall not entertain any appeal against the Order made by the Debts Recovery Tribunal under section 17, unless 50% of the amount of debt due is deposited with the Appellate Tribunal with a proviso that the Appellate Tribunal is vested with the discretion to reduce the amount to not less than 25% of the debt.

- The Recovery of Debts Due to Banks and Financial Institutions Act was also amended to include a proviso to section 19 (1) to the effect that the bank or financial institution may, with the permission of the Debts Recovery Tribunal, withdraw the application whether made before or after the Enforcement of Security Interest and Recovery of Debt Laws (Amendment) Act, 2004 for the purposes of taking action under the SARFAESI Act. The interpretation of this proviso came for consideration in a subsequent case decided by the Hon'ble Supreme Court, in the matter of Transcore Vs Union of India.(discussed in detail separately)

2. CLASSIFICATION OF ACCOUNT AS NPA-LEGAL VALIDITY

The classification of the account of the borrowers as 'NPA' by Banks under the Sarfaesi Act has been taken up as an issue of dispute between the Bank and the borrowers in various Courts/Judicial Forums. Several rounds of litigation has happend on this issue at various courts across the country. Ultimately, now the Hon'ble Supreme Court of India settled this issue in its latest judgement delivered on 28th January,2015 in Keshavlal Khemchand and Sons Pvt. Ltd Vs. Union of India & Others[32], by upholding the constitutional validity of the amended definition of the expression 'NPA' under Section 2(1)(o) of the Sarfaesi Act.

The original definiion of NPA as given under the provisions of the Sarfaesi Act, 2002 and the amended definition of NPA after the amendment act passed in 2004, which is now under challenge are given below for better understanding of the issue:-

Definition of NPA as under Sarfaesi Act,2002

Definition of NPA after Sarfaesi Amendment

Act,2004

Section 2(1) (o) - "non-performing asset" means an asset or account of a borrower, which has been classified by a bank or financial institution as sub-standard, doubtful or loss asset in accordance with the directions or under guidelines relating to assets classifications issued by the Reserve Bank.

Section 2(1) (o) - "non-performing asset" means an asset or account of a borrower, which has been classified by a bank or financial institution as sub-standard, doubtful or loss asset -

(a) in case such bank or financial institution is

administered or regulated by any authority or body established, constituted or appointed by

[32] Keshavlal Khemchand and Sons Pvt. Ltd Vs. Union of India & Others, Writ Petition (Civil) No.901 of 2014

any law for the time being in force, in accordance with the directions or guidelines relating to assets classifications issued by such authority or body;

(b) in any other case, in accordance with the directions or guidelines relating to assets

classifications issued by the Reserve Bank.

While challenging the constitutionality of the amended definition of the expression 'NPA' under Section 2(1)(o) of the Sarfaesi Act, the borrowers raised inter alia the following contentions before the Hon'ble Supreme Court of India:-

1. The Parliamnet abdicated its essential legislative function by authorising the various bodies to frame guidelines in accordance with which the account of the borrower could be classified as NPA.
2. 2. The amended definition of NPA enables different Creditors to adopt different guidelines which prescribe different standards for arriving at a conclusion that the account of a borrower is NPA.
3. The Sarfaesi Act does not provide for a reasonable opportunity to demonstrate that the classification of the borrower's account as NPA is untenable, the power to make such a classification itself becomes arbitrary and violative of Article 14 of the Constitution.

In responding to these contentions, the Union of India, RBI and Bankers have taken the following stand before the Hon'ble Supreme Court of India:-

1. Since the assessment of an account of borrower as NPA depends upon innumerable factors which constantly keep changing, Parliamnet thought it fit to stipulate that the assessment be made in the light of the guidelines made by either the RBI or various other Regulators regulating the activities of various creditors. Hence, there is no delegation of any essential legislative functions.
2. The classification of NPA on the basis of the guidelines framed by different bodies regulating the different creditors is a constitutionally permissible classification having regard to

the nature of the different credit facilities extended by various creditors to different categories of borrowers and on different terms and conditions. During the course of arguments, the Reserve Bank of India submitted that prior to the amendments in 2004, NPA was defined as sub-standard, doubtful or loss asset in accordance with the directions or under guidelines relating to assets classification issued by the Reserve Bank. Irrespective of whether the financial entity was regulated by RBI or not, for the purposes of Sarfaesi Act, the asset classification stipulated by RBI was applicable. Though the regulator concerned of the financial entity had stipulated different standards for regulatory purposes, the entities had to apply the criteria stipulated by RBI for asset classification so far as Sarfaesi Act was concerned. The amendment brought in 2004, addresses this issue and brings in uniformity in the classification of assets by financial entities, both for the purposes of complying with the directions issued by their own regulations and for the purposes of Sarfaesi Act. Thus, the amendement in 2004, ruled out a situation where an asset is not an NPA as per the specifications of the regulator but the same asset is an NPA for the purposes of Sarfaesi Act or vice versa.

The Department of Financial Services, Ministry of Finance also submitted before the Hon'ble Court that the amendements were made in 2004 to ensure that the guidelines issued by the concerned regulator are covered for the purpose of recovery under the Sarfaesi Act. It is further amendments in 2004, NPA was defined as sub-standard, doubtful or loss asset in accordance with the directions or under guidelines relating to assets classification issued by the Reserve Bank. Irrespective of whether the financial entity was regulated by RBI or not, for the purposes of Sarfaesi Act, the asset classification stipulated by RBI was applicable. Though the regulator concerned of the financial entity had stipulated different standards for regulatory purposes, the entities had to apply the criteria stipulated by RBI for asset classification so far as Sarfaesi Act was concerned. The amendment brought in 2004, addresses this issue and brings in uniformity in the classification of assets by financial entities, both for the purposes of complying with the directions issued by their own regulations and for the purposes of Sarfaesi Act. Thus, the amendement in 2004, ruled out a situation where an asset is not an NPA as per the specifications of the regulator but the same asset is an NPA for the purposes of Sarfaesi Act or vice versa.

The Department of Financial Services, Ministry of Finance also submitted before the Hon'ble Court that the amendements were made in 2004 to ensure that the guidelines issued by

the concerned regulator are covered for the purpose of recovery under the Sarfaesi Act. It is further submitted that there are financial institutions such as Housing Finance Corporations, which are regulated by National Housing Bank. The non-performing assets of these institutions are classified as per the guidelines prescribed by National Housing Bank. The amendment covered the entities regulated by different regulators such as RBI, National Housing Bank, Asian Development Bank. Therefore, the amendments were necessary to cover the deficiencies noticed in the Sarfaesi Act. Taking into account of the arguments extended on behalf of RBI, Ministry of Finance and the Bankers, the Hon'ble Supreme Court of India held that the allegations of the borrowers that the Sarfaesi Act does not provide for a reasonable opportunity to demonstrate that the classification of the borrower's account as NPA fail on the express language of Section 13(3A), which obligates the Secured Creditors (Banks) to examine the representation/objection made by the borrower and communicate the reasons for non-acceptance of the representation or objecctions to the borrowers.

In view of the aforesaid observations, the Hon'ble Supreme Court upheld that the amended definition of the expression "NPA" under Section 2(1)(o) of the Act as constitutionally valid. Accordingly, the Hon'ble Supreme Court allowed the appeals filed by the Creditors/Banks and also directed each petitioner/borrower to pay costs to the respective Creditors/Banks calculated at 1% of the amount outstanding on the date of notice under Section 13(2) of the Act in each of the cases. The legal validity of the provisions relating to the classification of the account as NPA and the RBI guidelines on this aspect was also considered by the Hon'ble High Court of Madras in M/s.Decan Chronicles Holdings Limited vs. Union of India and others[33]. The Hon'ble Court observed that what is required to be seen is the intention of the Legislature at the time of enactment. In this case, the Legislature has left the job of defining "non-performing asset" in the hands of Reserve Bank of India. The Reserve Bank of India has issued the Master Circular on NPA after taking into consideration of the global economy, the prevailing situation, the intention to create transparency and uniformity with the Banking system to provide stability and to protect the interests of depositors. When such a decision has been made based upon analysis of material factors, the same cannot be set aside as arbitrary.

The Reserve Bank of India has laid down a policy providing guidelines in the matter for declaring an asset to be a non-performing asset known as "RBIs prudential norms on income

[33] M/s.Decan Chronicles Holdings Limited Vs. Union of India and others, W.P.No.5897/2014.

recognition, asset classification and provisioning-pertaining to advances" through a Circular dated 30-8-2001. In the said circular, it is mentioned as follows: on the Financial System (Chairman Shri M. Narasimham), the Reserve Bank of India has introduced, in a phased manner, prudential norms for income recognition, asset classification and provisioning for the advances portfolio of the banks so as to move towards greater consistency and transparency in the published accounts."

2.1 Non-performing Assets:

"2.1.1 An asset, including a leased asset, becomes non-performing when it ceases to generate income for the bank. A non-performing asset (NPA) was defined as a credit facility in respect of which the interest and/or installment of principal has remained past due for a specified period of time. The specified period was reduced in a phased manner as under:

Accordingly, as from that date, a Non-performing Asset (NPA) shall be an advance where:

   i.   interest and/or instalment of principal remain overdue for a period of more than 180 days in respect of a Term Loan,
  ii.   the account remains out of order for a period of more than 180 days, in respect of an Overdraft/Cash Credit (OD/CC),
  iii.   the bill remains overdue for a period of more than 180 days in the case of bills purchased and

discounted,

  iv.   interest and/or instalment of principal remains overdue for two harvest seasons but for a period

not exceeding two and half years in the case of an advance granted for agricultural purposes, and

  v.   any amount to be received remains overdue for a period of more than 180 days in respect of other accounts. (Subsequently as per the instructions of RBI, 180 days was reduced to 90 days.

4.2.2 Banks should establish appropriate internal systems to eliminate the tendency to delay or postpone the identification of NPAs, especially in respect of high value accounts. The banks may fix a minimum cut off point to decide what would constitute a high value account depending upon

their respective business levels. The cut off point should be valid for the entire accounting year. Responsibility and validation levels for ensuring proper asset classification may be fixed by the banks. The system should ensure that doubts in asset classification due to any reason are settled

through specified internal channels within one month from the date on which the account would have been classified as NPA as per extant guidelines."

The Hon'ble Court held that from what is quoted above, the Reserve Bank of India has lay down the terms and conditions and circumstances in which the debt is to be classified as non- performing asset and hence there is no substance in the submission made on behalf of the petitioners that there are no guidelines for treating the debt as a non-performing asset.

It is relevant to add that the Narasimham Committee also advocates for a legal framework which may clearly define the rights and liabilities of the parties to the contract and provisions for speedy resolution of disputes, which is a sine qua non for efficient trade and commerce, especially for financial intermediation. Even the guidelines of the Reserve Bank of India in relation to classifying the NPAs says, a system be evolved which should ensure that the doubts in asset classification are settled or resolved through specified internal channels within the time specified in the guidelines. It is thus clear that while recommending speedier steps for recovery of the debts it is envisaged by all concerned authorities that within the legal framework, relevant provisions may be contained which may curtail the delays.ThE circular also provides for sale of the financial assets on 'without recourse' basis and the Banks were directed to ensure that the effect of the sale of the financial assets should be such that the asset is taken off the books of the Bank and after the sale there should not be any known liability devolving on the Banks. The guideline procedure for sale of bank's financial assets to the Securitisation/ Reconstruction Companies has been laid down by the Reserve Bank of India in the Master Circular issued on

July1, 2014[34].

3.   MECHANISM TO RESOLVE LEGAL ISSUES –CHALLENGES

As regards the mechanism to resolve the issues relating to classification of accounts as Non- Performing Assets, the borrower/ guarantor is entitled to submit objections and representations under section 13(3A) of the Act. The purpose of serving a notice upon the borrower under subsection (2) of section 13 of the Act is that a reply may be submitted by the borrower explaining the reasons as to why measures may or may not be taken under sub-section (4) of section 13 in case of non-compliance of notice within 60 days. The Authorised Officer is legally

[34] RBI Mater Circular no.DBOD.No.BP.BC.9/21.04.048/2014-15 dated July 1, 2014.

bound to apply its mind to the objections raised in reply to such notice and an internal mechanism must be particularly evolved to consider such objections raised in the reply to the notice.

In terms of the Judgement of the Hon'ble Supreme Court in Mardia Chemicals case, there must be some meaningful consideration of the objections raised rather than to ritually reject them and proceed to take drastic measures under sub-section (4) of section 13 of the Act. Once such a duty is envisaged on the part of the creditor it would only be conducive to the principles of fairness on the part of the banks and financial institutions in dealing with their borrowers to apprise them of the reason for not accepting the objections or points raised in reply to the notice served upon them before proceeding to take measures under sub-section (4) of section 13. Such reasons, overruling the objections of the borrower, must also be communicated to the borrower by the secured creditor.

While stressing the need for proper consideration of the objections of the borrowers/guarantors, the Hon'ble Court also made it clear unequivocally that communication of the reasons not accepting the objections taken by the secured borrower may not be taken to give an occasion to resort to such proceedings which are not permissible under the provisions of the Act. But communication of reasons not to accept the objections of the borrower, would certainly be for the purpose of his knowledge which would be a step forward towards his right to know as to why his objections have not been accepted by the secured creditor who intends to resort to harsh steps of taking over the management/business of viz. secured assets without intervention of the Court. Such a person in respect of whom steps under section 13(4) of the Act are likely to be taken cannot be denied the right to know the reason of non-acceptance and of his objections. It is true as per the provisions under the Act, he may not be entitled to challenge the reasons communicated or the likely action of the secured creditor at that point of time unless his right to approach the Debt Recovery Tribunal as provided under section 17 of the Act matures on any measure having been taken under sub-section (4) of section 13 of the Act.

4. IMPORTANCE OF COMMUNICATING REASONS FOR REJECTION OF REPRESENTATION/OBJECTION UNDER SECTION 3 (3A) OF SARFAESI ACT

In terms of Section 3 (3A) of the Sarfaesi Act, it is necessary to communicate the reasons for not accepting the objections raised by the borrower in reply to notice under section 13(2) of

the Act. Therefore, it goes with logic and reason that the borrower/guarantor may communicate the reason for not accepting the objections, if raised and before takes the measures like taking over possession of the secured assets, etc.

This will also be in tune with the concept of right to know and lenders liability of fairness to keep the borrower informed particularly the developments immediately before taking measures under sub-section (4) of section 13 of the Act. It will also cater the cause of transparency and shall be conducive in building an atmosphere of confidence and healthy commercial practice. Such a duty is inherent under section 13(2) of the Act.

5. RIGHT TO FILE APPEAL BEFORE DRT

The next safeguard available to a secured borrower within the framework of the Act is to approach the Debt Recovery Tribunal under section 17 of the Act. Such a right accrues only after measures are taken under sub-section (1) of section 13 of the Act. The Section 13 of the Act leaves more scope and provides wider protection to the borrower as compared to in the case of English mortgage. In English mortgage, there is no scope of intervention of the court unless a case is made out before the court that action of the mortgagee is fraudulent or it is a case of the like nature. Otherwise as provided under sub-section (3) of section 69 a mortgagor shall only be entitled to the damages for the wrongful or irregular sale of the property. Whereas under the Securitisation rules it is provided that before putting the property on sale the authorized officer has to obtain the valuation of immovable property, a reserved price is to be fixed and a notice of 30 days before sale is to be served on the borrower. In this connection, rule 9, the relevant rule, of the Security Interest (Enforcement) Rules, 2002 is quoted:

"9. Time of sale, issues of sale certificate and delivery of possession, etc.

1. No sale of immovable property under these rules shall take place before the expiry of thirty days from the date on which the public notice of sale is published in newspapers as referred to in the proviso to sub-rule (6) or notice of sale has been served to the borrower.
2. The sale shall be confirmed in favour of the purchaser who has offered the highest sale price in his bid or tender or quotation or offer to the authorized officer and shall be subject to confirmation by the secured creditor."

Therefore, during this period which would be more than 60 days it would be open for a borrower to approach the Debt Recovery Tribunal and file a petition for any appropriate relief and if a case

is so made out, he can even get a relief of stay, in exercise of ancillary power which vest in the Tribunal as per decisions referred and ITO v. Mohd Kunhi[35]and, Allahabad Bank v. Radha Krishna Maity[36].

In terms of section 19 of the Act, if the Tribunal finds that the secured assets have been wrongfully transferred or taken possession, an order for return of such assets can be passed and the borrower in that even shall also be entitled for compensation.

A full reading of section 34 shows that the jurisdiction of the civil court is barred in respect of matters which a Debt Recovery Tribunal or Appellate Tribunal is empowered to determine in respect of any action taken "or to be taken in pursuance of any power conferred under this Act". In this context the judgement of Hon'ble High Court of Calcutta in **M/s.Mercury Exporters and Manufacturing Pvt. Ltd & Anr. Vs. Punjab National Bank and Anr** [37] . is worth mentioning. The Hon'ble Calcutta High Court held that the borrowers/guarantors can approach the Debt Recovery Tribunal under Section 17(1) of the Act only after possession of the secured asset is lost by the borrower/guarantor.

6. APPELLATE PROCEEDINGS – A MISNOMER

In terms of judgements of various courts, the proceedings under section 17 of the Act, are not appellate proceedings and it is a misnomer. In fact it is the initial action which is brought before a Forum as prescribed under the Act, raising grievance against the action or measures taken by one of the parties to the contract. It is the stage of initial proceeding like filing a suit in civil court. As a matter of fact, proceedings under section 17 of the Act are in lieu of a civil suit which remedy is ordinarily available but for the bar under section 34 of the Act in the present case.

The Hon'ble Court referred to the decision in Smt. Ganga Bai v. Vijay Kumar[38] where in respect of original and appellate proceedings a distinction has been drawn as follows:

"15 ... There is a basic distinction between the right of suit and the right of appeal. There is an inherent right in every person to bring a suit of civil nature and unless the suit is barred by statute one may, at ones peril, bring a suit of one's choice. It is no answer to a suit, howsoever frivolous

[35] ITO v. Mohd Kunhi (1969) 2 SCR 65

[36] Allahabad Bank v. Radha Krishna Maity (1999) 6 SCC 755

[37] M/s.Mercury Exporters and Manufacturing Pvt. Ltd & Anr. Vs. Punjab National Bank and Anr. W.P.No.353 of 2014

[38] Smt. Ganga Bai v. Vijay Kumar (1974) 2 SCC 393

to claim, that the law confers no such right to sue. A suit for its maintainability requires no authority of law and it is enough that no statute bars the suit. But the position in regard to appeals is quite the opposite. The right of appeal inheres in no one and, therefore, an appeal for its maintainability must have the clear authority of law. That explains why the right of appeal is described as a creature of statute." (p. 397)

7. PRE-DEPOSIT OF 75% FOR FILING APPEAL

The Hon'ble Supreme Court in Mardia Chemicals case[39] held that the requirement of predeposit of any amount at the first instance of proceedings is not to be found in any of the decisions of the Superior Courts. The amount of deposit of 75 per cent of the demand, at the initial proceeding itself sounds unreasonable and oppressive more particularly when the secured assets/the management thereof along with the right to transfer such interest has been taken over by the secured creditor or in some cases property is also sold. The requirement of deposit of such a heavy amount on basis of one sided claim alone, cannot be said to be a reasonable condition at the first instance itself before start of adjudication of the dispute. Merely giving power to the Tribunal to waive or reduce the amount, does not cure the inherent infirmity leaning one-sidedly in favour of the party, who, so far has alone been the party to decide the amount and the fact of default and classifying the dues as NPAs without participation/association of the borrower in the process. Such an onerous and oppressive condition should not be left operative in expectation of reasonable exercise of discretion by the concerned authority. Placed in a situation as indicated above, where it may not be possible for the borrower to raise any amount to make the deposit, his secured assets having already been taken possession of or sold, such a rider to approach the Tribunal at the first instance of proceedings, captioned as appeal, renders the remedy illusory and nugatory.

As indicated earlier, the position of the appeal under section 17 of the Act is like that of a suit in the court of the first instance under the Code of Civil Procedure. No doubt in suits also it is permissible, in given facts and circumstances and under the provisions of the law to attach the property before a decree is passed or to appoint a receiver and to make a provision by way of interim measure in respect of the property in suit. But for obtaining such orders a case for the

[39] Mardia Chemicals - Mardia Chemicals Ltd V Union of India AIR 2004 SC 2371

same is to be made out in accordance with the relevant provisions under the law. There is no such provision under the Act.

The justification given by Bank's /FI's regarding the requirement of pre-deposit is that the secured assets which may be taken possession of or sold may fall short of the dues, therefore, such a deposit may be necessary. However, the Hon'ble Court find no merit in this submission. In such an eventuality, the recourse may have to be taken to sub-section 10 of section 13 where a petition may have to be filed before the Tribunal for the purpose of making up of the short-fall.

The condition of pre-deposit in the present case is bad rendering the remedy illusory on the grounds that (i) it is imposed while approaching the adjudicating authority of the first instance, not in appeal, (ii) there is no determination of the amount due as yet (iii) the secured assets or its management with transferable interest is already taken over and under control of the secured creditor (iv) no special reason for double security in respect of an amount yet to be determined and settled (v) 75 per cent of the amount claimed by no means would be a meager amount (vi) it will leave the borrower in a position where it would not be possible for him to raise any funds to make deposit of 75 per cent of the undetermined demand. Such conditions are not alone onerous and oppressive but also unreasonable and arbitrary and held sub-section (2) of section 17 of the Act as unreasonable, arbitrary and violative of article 14 of the Constitution.

8. PUBLIC INTEREST VERSUS PRIVATE INTEREST

One of the contentions which have been forcefully raised against the SARFAESI Act is that the existing rights of private parties under a contract cannot be interfered with, more particularly putting one party to an advantageous position over the other. For example, in the matter of private contract between the borrower and the financing bank or institution through impugned legislation rights of the borrowers have been curtailed and enforcement of secured assets has been provided for without intervention of the court and above all depriving them the remedy available under the law by approaching to the civil court. Such a law, it is submitted, is not envisaged in any civilized society governed by rule of law.

The Hon'ble Supreme Court held in Mardia Chemicals case that though the transaction may have a character of a private contract yet the question of great importance behind such transactions as a whole having far reaching effect on the economy of the country cannot be ignored, purely

restricting it to individual transactions more particularly when financing is through banks and financial institutions utilizing the money of the people in general namely, the depositors in the banks and public money at the disposal of the financial institutions.

Therefore, wherever public interest to such a large extent is involved and it may become necessary to achieve an object which serves the public purposes, individual rights may have to give way. Public interest has always been considered to be above the private interest. The interest of individual may, to some extent, be affected but it cannot have the potential of taking over the public interest having an impact in the socio-economic drive of the country. The two aspects are inter-twined which are difficult to be separated. There have been many instances where existing rights of the individuals have been affected by legislative measures taken in public interest. In Ramaswamy Aiyengar v. Kailasa Thevar[40]1951, by enacting the Madras Agriculturalists Relief Act, relief was given to the debtors who were agriculturists as a class, by sealing down their debts. The validity of the Act was upheld though it affected the individual interest of creditors.

In the **Dahya Lal v. Rasul Mohd. Abdul Rahim**[41](1963) 3 SCR 1, the tenants under the Provisions of the Bombay Tenancy Act, 1939 were given protection against eviction and they were granted the status of protected tenant, who had cultivated the land personally six years prior to the prescribed date. It was found that the legislation was with the object of improving the economic condition of the peasants and for ensuring full and efficient use of land for agricultural purpose. In the case of Kanshi Ram v. Lachhman[42] (2001) 5 SCC 546 the law granting relief to the debtors protecting their property was upheld.

The Hon'ble Court further held that in the present case, the unrealized dues of banking companies and financial institutions utilizing public money for advances were mounting and it was considered imperative in view of recommendations of experts committees to have such law which may provide speedier remedy before any major fiscal set back occurs and for improvement of general financial flow of money necessary for the economy of the country that the impugned Act was enacted. Such legislation would be in the public interest and the individual interest shall be subservient to it. Even if a few borrowers are affected here and there, that would not impinge upon the validity of the Act which otherwise serves the larger interest.

[40] Ramaswamy Aiyengar v. Kailasa Thevar 1951 SCR 292.

[41] Dahya Lal v. Rasul Mohd. Abdul Rahim (1963) 3 SCR

[42] Kanshi Ram v. Lachhman (2001) 5 SCC 546

9.   INDEPENDENT ADJUDICATORY AUTHORITY

Another manor conention against the SARFAESI Act is that no adjudicatory mechanism is available to the borrower to ventilate his grievance through an independent adjudicatory authority. Access to the justice is the hall-mark of our judicial system. Section 34 of the Act bars the jurisdiction of the civil courts to entertain a suit in matters of recovery of loans. The remedy of appeal available under the Act as contained in section 17 can be availed only after measures have already been taken by the secured creditor under sub-section (4) of section 13 of the Act which includes sale of the secured assets, taking over its management and all transferable rights thereto. Before filing an appeal under section 17 of the Act, decision is to be taken in respect of all matters by the bank or financial institution itself which can hardly be said to be an independent agency rather they are a party to the transaction having unilateral power to initiate action under sub-section (4) of section 13 of the Act. The remedy under article 226 of the Constitution of India may not always be available since the dispute may be only between two private parties, the banking companies, co-operative Banks or financial institutions, foreign banks, some of them may not be authorities within the meaning of article 12 of the Constitution of India against whom a writ petition could be maintainable. Thus the position that emerges is that a borrower is virtually left with no remedy. Where access to the court is prohibited and no proper adjudicatory mechanism is provided such a law is unconstitutional and cannot survive[43]. Some adjudicatory process through an independent agency is essential for determining the rights of the parties more particularly when the consequences which flow from the offending Act defeat the civil rights of a party[44].

The Bankers maintained the stand that in a contractual matter between the two private parties they are supposed to act in terms of the contract and no question of compliance with the principles of natural justice arises nor the question of judicial review of such actions need to be provided for. However, the Hon'ble Court held in Mardia Chemicals case[45] that contract which has been entered into between the two private parties, in some respects has been superseded by the statutory provisions or it may be said that such contracts are now governed by the statutory provisions relating to recovery of debts and bar of jurisdiction of the civil court to entertain any

[43] 1L. Chandrakumar v. Union of India (1997) 3 SCC 261

[44] Surya Dev Rai v. Ram Chander Rai (2003) 6 SCC 675.

[45] Mardia Chemicals - Mardia Chemicals Ltd V Union of India AIR 2004 SC 2371

dispute in respect of such matters. Hence, it cannot be pleaded that the petitioners cannot complaint of the conduct of the banking companies and financial institutions for whatever goes in between the two is absolutely a matter of contract between private parties, therefore, no adjudication may be necessary.

Hence, after taking into consideration all the aspects involved in the case the Hon'ble Supreme Court upheld all the provisions of the SARFAESI Act except, the requirement of deposit of 75 per cent of amount claimed before entertaining an appeal (petition) under section 17 of the Act is an oppressive, onerous and arbitrary condition against all the canons of reasonableness and strike down the same.

The Hon'ble Court further held that the borrowers would get a reasonably fair deal and opportunity to get the matter adjudicated upon before the Debt Recovery Tribunal. The effect of some of the provisions may be a bit harsh for some of the borrowers but on that ground the impugned provisions of the Act cannot be said to be unconstitutional in view of the fact that the object of the Act is to achieve speedier recovery of the dues declared as NPAs and better availability of capital liquidity and resources to help in growth of economy of the country and welfare of the people in general which would subserve the public interest.

Accordingly, the Hon'ble High Court upholds the validity of the Act and its provisions except that of sub-section (2) of section 17 of the Act, which is declared ultra vires of article 14 of the Constitution of India. The Hon'ble Court further observed that where a secured creditor has taken action under Section 13(4) of the Act, it would be open to borrowers to file appeals under section 17 of the Act within the limitation as prescribed, therefore, to be counted with effect from today.

In the light of the above discussion, it can be summarised that the constitutionality of the provisions of both the Recovery of Debts Due to Banks and Financial Institutions Act and the Securitisation and Reconstruction of Financial Assets and Enforcement of Security Interest Act have been upheld by the Hon'ble Supreme except the Section 17(2) of the SARFAESI Act, which was strike down by the Supreme Court as arbitrary and unconstitutional.

CHAPTER – 5

ROLE OF JUDICIARY IN INTERPRETING AND ESTABLISHING RECOVERY LAWS RELATING TO BANKING INSTITUTIONS

"Law, without force, is impotent".

Blaise Pascal (1623-1662) French mathematician, physicist and philosopher

The Banks and Financial Institutions operating in our country are required to comply with all the laws & rules laid down in various Indian statutes such as Banking Regulations Act, Reserve Bank of India Act, Indian Contract Act, Transfer of Property Act, SARFAESI Act, DRT Act, etc. Apart from the laws & rules laid down in the statutes, the Banks and Financial Institutions are equally bound to follow the judgments of the Supreme Court and High Courts which are also laws of the land. In terms of Article 141 of the Constitution of India, judgments delivered by the Supreme Court of India are laws and binding precedents on all Banking and Financial Institutions operating in our country. Of late, the Supreme Courts and High Courts are passing judgements, which are of high important & relevant to the area of operations today. The judgments' of the Supreme Court in Mardia Chemicals Ltd v Union of India & Others47 and in Transcore v Union of India and Anr48 are few instances of such landmark judgments' on this point. In fact, the judgement in Mardia Chemicals case upholds the constitutionality of the SARFEASI Act, whereby the Bank's/FI's were allowed to act independently without approaching the courts of law. Further, the judgment in Transcore case empowered the Bank's/FI's to initiate simultaneously proceedings both under the SAREASI Act & DRT Act.

In this chapter, the legal implications of various judgements of the Hon'ble Supreme Court and High Courts pertaining to the laws with respect to the recovery of dues to the Banks and Financial Institutions with special reference to Sarfaesi Act and how such judgements helped in devolving the present legal system will be discussed in detail.

1. MARDIA CHEMICALS LTD VUNION OF INDIA & OTHERS

In the landmark judgement delivered in Mardia Chemicals Ltd V Union of India[46] the Hon'ble Supreme Court of India held that the provisions of the Securitisation and Reconstruction of Financial Assets and Enforcement of Security Interest Act, 2002 (hereinafter referred to as SARFEASI Act) are valid except sub-section (2) of section 17, which is ultra vires of Article 14 of the Constitution of India.

1. The main contention of the petitioner borrower:

The petitioner challenged the constitutional validity of the SARFEASI Act. The main contention challenging the vires of the provisions of the Act was that the Banks and the Financial Institutions have been vested with arbitrary powers, without guidelines for its exercise and also without providing any appropriate and adequate mechanism to decide the disputes relating to the correctness of the demand, its validity and the actual amount of the dues, sought to be recovered from the borrowers. The further contentions put forwarded by the petitioner are as follows:-

- That the SARFEASI Act has been made one sided affair while enforcing drastic measures of sale of the property or taking over the management of the possession of the secured assets without affording any opportunity to the borrower.
- That there was no occasion to enact such a draconian legislation to find a short-cut to realize the dues, without borrower's ascertainment but only on the basis on which the secured creditor considered the dues and declare the same as non-performing assets (NPAs).
- That there is already a special enactment providing for recovery of dues of Banks and Financial Institutions i.e. DRT Act.

That no provision has been made to take into account the lender's liability, though at one time it was considered necessary to have an enactment relating to lender's liability and a bill was also intended to be introduced, as it was considered that it is necessary for the lender's as well to conduct themselves responsibly towards the borrowers. Neither any such law has been enacted so far, nor has any care been taken to introduce such safeguards in the SARFEASI Act to protect the borrowers against their vulnerability to

[46]Mardia Chemicals Ltd v Union of India & Others (2004 D.R.T.C 1(SC)

arbitrary or irresponsible action on the part of the lenders. The mechanism provided for recovery of the debt under section 13 does not provide for any adjudicatory forum to resolve any dispute which may arise in relation to the liability of the borrower to be treated as a defaulter or to see as to whether there has been any violation or lapse on the part of the creditor or in regard to the correctness of the amount sought to be recovered and the interest levied thereupon.

- That the provision of appeal contained in section 17 of the SARFEASI Act is illusory since the appeal would be maintainable after the possession of the property or the management of the secured assets has been taken over or the property has been sold. Further, appeal is not entertainable unless 75 percentage of the amount claimed in the notice is deposited by the borrower with the Debt Recovery Tribunal.

1 (b). The main contention of the respondent bank:

The respondents primarily the Banks put forward the following line of arguments in favour of enactment of the SARFEASI Act:-

- The SAREASI Act was enacted to curb the menace of growing non-performing assets (NPAs). It affects the banks and financial institutions, which is ultimately against the public interest. Since, the recovery through DRT was not encouraging, need was felt for a faster procedure empowering the secured creditors to recover their dues and for securitization of financial assets so as to generate maximum monetary liquidity.
- In case, the borrower wants to raise any objection against section 13(2) of the SARFEASI Act, it may be raised in reply to the notice which would obviously be considered by the secured creditor before it would further proceed to take recourse to sub-section 4 of section 13 of the Act. So an opportunity has been provided to the borrower under the provisions of the Act.
- The proviso to section 17 very clearly provides that on an application, the condition of deposit of amount can be waived or the amount can be reduced. Therefore, it would not be correct to say that condition of pre-deposit is harsh as it can relaxed in deserving cases.

iv. The bar of jurisdiction of the Civil Court was thought to be necessary to avoid lengthy legal process in realizing the amount due.

1 (c). The main questions for consideration by the court:

Taking the overall view of the rival contentions of the parties in the case, the Hon'ble court draw the following main questions for consideration:-

I. Whether it is open to challenge the statute on the ground that it was not necessary to enact it in the prevailing background particularly when another statute was already in operation?
II. Whether provisions as contained under section 13 and 17 of the act provide adequate and efficacious mechanism to consider and decide the objections/disputes raised by a borrower against the recovery, particularly in view of bar to approach the Civil

Court under section 34 of the Act?

III. Whether the remedy available under section 17 of the Act is illusory for the reason it is available only after the action is taken under section 13(4) of the Act and the appeal would be entertainable only on deposit of 75 per cent of the claim raised in the notice of demand?

IV. Whether the terms or existing rights under the contract entered into by two private parties could be amended by the provisions of law providing certain powers in one-sided manner in favour of one of the parties to the contract?

V. Whether provision for sale of the properties without intervention of the Court under section

13 of the Act is akin to the English mortgage and its effect on the scope of the bar of the jurisdiction of the Civil Court?

VI. Whether the provisions under section 13 and 17(2) of the Act are unconstitutional on the basis of the parameters laid down in different decisions of this Court?

VII. Whether the principle of lender's liability has been absolutely ignored while enacting the Act and its effect?

1 (d). The ratio of judgment of the court:

As regard the first question, the Hon'ble Court held that in the present day of global economy it may be difficult to stick to old and conventional methods of financing and recovery of dues. Hence, it cannot be said that a step taken towards securitization of the debts and to evolve means for faster recovery of the NPA's was not called for or that it was superimposition of the undesired law since one legislation was already operating in the field namely the Recovery of Debts Due to Banks and Financial Institutions Act. Considering the totality of circumstances the financial climate world over, if it was thought as a matter of policy, to have yet speedier legal method to recover the dues, such a policy decision cannot be faulted with nor it is a matter to be gone into by the Courts to test the legitimacy of such a measure relating to financial policy.

With respect to the question no.02, the Hon'ble Court held that a policy has been laid down by the Reserve Bank of India providing guidelines in the matter for declaring an asset to be a nonperforming asset known as "RBI's prudential norms on income recognition, asset classification and provisioning pertaining to advances". In terms of the RBI's circular, an asset, including a leased asset, becomes non-performing when it ceases to generate income for the bank. Since the terms and conditions and circumstances in which the debt is to be classified as non-performing asset has been laid down by the Reserve Bank of India, the Hon'ble Court find no substance in the submission of the petitioners that there are no guidelines for treating the debt as a non-performing asset.

While dealing with the third question, the Hon'ble Court held that the amount of deposit of 75 per cent of the demand, at the initial proceedings itself, sounds unreasonable and oppressive. Requirement of deposit of such a heavy amount on basis of one sided claim alone, cannot be said to be a reasonable condition at the first instance itself before start of adjudication of the dispute. Merely giving power to the Tribunal to waive or reduce the amount, does not cure the inherent infirmity leaning one-sidedly in favour of the party, who, so far has alone been the party to decide the amount and the fact of default and classifying the dues a NPAs without participation/association of the borrower in the process.

As regards the fourth question, the Hon'ble Court held that though the transaction may have a character of a private contract yet the question of great importance behind such transaction as a whole having far reaching effect on the economy of the country cannot be ignored, purely restricting it to individual transactions more particularly when financing is through banks and

financial institutions utilizing the money of the people in general namely, the depositors in the banks and public money at the disposal of the financial institutions. Therefore, wherever public interest to such a large extent is involved and it may become necessary to achieve an object which serves the public purposes, individual rights may have to give way. Public interest has always been considered to be above the private interest.

While dealing with the fifth question, the Hon'ble Court held that section 13 of the SARFEASI Act overrides the provisions contained in section 69 of the Transfer of Property Act, where it is said that in no cases, other than those as enumerated in clause (a), (b) and (c) of section 69, a mortgage shall be enforced without the intervention of the Court. Once the condition given in section 69 of the TP Act, the general law on the subject, has been overridden by the special enactment, namely, the Securitization Act, it would not make much of a difference as to whether the transactions in question are akin to or amount to English mortgage or not, since irrespective of the kind of the mortgage, the secured interest is liable to be enforced without intervention of the Court as per the provision contained under section 13 of the Act.

While addressing the sixth & seventh questions, the Hon'ble Court held that on measures having been taken under sub-section (4) of section 13 and before the date of sale /auction of the property it would be open for the borrower to file an appeal under section 17 of the SAREASI Act before the Debt Recovery Tribunal. After service of 13(2) notice, if the borrower raises any objection or places facts for consideration of the secured creditor, such reply to the notice must be considered with due application of mind and the reasons for not accepting the objections, however brief they may be, must be communicated to the borrower. The Hon'ble Court held that the effect of some of the provisions may be a bit harsh for some of the borrowers but on that ground the impugned provisions of the SARFEASI Act cannot be said to be unconstitutional in view of the fact that the object of the Act is to achieve speedier recovery of the dues declared as NPAs and better availability of capital liquidity and resources to help in growth of economy of the country and welfare of the people in general which would sub serve the public interest. In this connection, the

Hon'ble Court also referred to the observations made in Collector of Customs, Madras v. Nathella Samapathu[47] wherein it was held that the intent of the Parliament shall not be defeated

[47] Collector of Customs, Madras v. Nathella Samapathu Collector of Customs, Madras v. Nathella Samapathu reported in 1962 (3) SCR 786 at pp.829-30.

merely for the reason that it may operate a bit harshly on a small section of public. In another decision i.e.Kishanchand Arora v. Commissioner of Police51 it was held that absence of appeal does not necessarily render the legislation unreasonable. However, the Hon'ble Court held that the requirement of deposit of 75 per cent of amount before entertaining an appeal under section

17 of the Act is an oppressive, onerous and arbitrary condition against all the cannons of reasonableness.

Such a condition is invalid and it is liable to be struck down. Accordingly, the Hon'ble Court upholds the validity of the SARFEASI Act and its provisions except that of sub-section (2) of section 17 of the Act, which is declared ultra vires of Article 14 of the Constitution of India.

TRANSCORE Vs. UNION OF INDIA AND ANOTHER

The Hon'ble Supreme Court of India in its landmark judgement in Transcore v Union of India and Anr[48] held that withdrawal of suit pending before DRT is not a pre-condition for taking recourse to the SARFEASI Act. This judgment is prominent in the sense that it cleared the legal conundrum regrarding the initiation of simultaneous proceedings under DRT Act and SARFAESI Act. This judgement permitted the Banks/FIs to proceed under the SARFEASI Act simultaneously without withdrawing the OA filed before DRT. The moot question, whether withdrawal of O.A. in terms of the first proviso to section 19(1) of the DRT Act, 1993 is a condition precedent to take recourse to the SARFEASI Act & Rules, 2002 has came for consideration before JJ. Arijit Pasayat and

S.H.Kapadia of the Hon'ble Supreme Court of India. The Hon'ble Supreme Court held that withdrawal of suit pending before DRT is not a pre- condition for taking recourse to the SARFEASI Act. The remedy under SARFEASI Act is additional remedy, which is not inconsistent with DRT Act, 1993 and therefore, doctrine of election has no application.

2 (a). The main contention of the petitioner borrower:

In this case, the Indian Overseas Bank, respondent herein, issued Possession Notice under Section 13(4) of the SARFEASI Act upon the appellant Company calling to repay the default

[48] Kishanchand Arora v. Commissioner of Police reported in 1961 (3) SCR 135

amount. The appellant Company contended that the respondent Bank could not have invoked the SARFEASI Act without the prior permission of the DRT before whom OA was pending. The appellant Company further contended that the respondent Bank is duty bound and obliged to make an application to the DRT seeking withdrawal of O.A. The first proviso to Section 19(1) of DRT Act states that the bank or financial institution may, with the permission of the DRT, on an application made by it, withdraw the O.A. made before or after the amending Act 30 of 2004 for the purpose of taking action under the SARFEASI Act, 2002, if no such action had been taken earlier under that Act.

2 (b). The main contention of the respondent bank:

The respondent Bank argued that the said proviso is an enabling provision; that banks and financial institutions have an independent right to recover debts; that the purpose behind enactment of the NPA Act was to obliterate all fetters on their right to recover the debt which earlier existed in the form of Sections 69 and 69A of the Transfer of Property Act, 1882, and consequently, the option lay with the banks/FI's to invoke or not to invoke the SARFEASI Act. The respondent Bank further argued that they were not mandatorily obliged to obtain the prior leave of DRT and that the said proviso is not a condition precedent to taking recourse to the NPA Act.

2 (c). The main questions for consideration by the court:

In this case, the Hon'ble Supreme Court settles the following points for determination:- ix. Whether the banks or financial institutions having elected to seek their remedy in terms of DRT Act, 1993 can still invoke the SARFEASI Act, 2002 for realizing the secured assets without withdrawing or abandoning the O.A filed before the DRT under the DRT Act?

x.   Whether recourse to take possession of the secured assets of the borrower in terms of section 13(4) of the SARFEASI Act comprehends the power to take actual possession of the immovable property?

xi.   Whether ad valorem court fee prescribed under rule 7 of the DRT (Procedure) Rules, 1993 is payable on an application under section 17(1) of the SARFEASI Act in the absence of any rule framed under the said Act?

At first, the Hon'ble Supreme Court examined the doctrine of election. The Hon'ble court held that there are three elements of election, namely, existence of two or more remedies; inconsistencies between such remedies and a choice of one of them. If any one of the three elements is not there, the doctrine will not apply. In the present case, the SARFEASI Act is an additional remedy to the DRT Act. Together they constitute one remedy and therefore, the doctrine of election does not apply. According to Snell's Equity, the doctrine of election of remedies is applicable only when there are two or more co-existent remedies available to the litigants at the time of election, which are repugnant and inconsistent. In any event, there is no repugnancy or inconsistency between the two remedies; therefore, the doctrine of election has no application.

The Hon'ble Court further held that the SARFEASI Act is enacted to enforce the interest in the financial assets which belongs to the bank/FI by virtue of the contract between the parties or by operation of common law principles or by law. The very object of section 13 of the SARFEASI Act is recovery by non-adjudicatory process. A secured asset under SARFEASI Act is an asset in which interest is created by the borrower in favour of the bank/FI and on that basis alone the SARFEASI Act seeks to enforce the security interest by non-adjudicatory process. The SARFEASI Act proceeds on the basis that the debtor has failed not only to repay the debt, but he has also failed to maintain the level of margin and to maintain value of the security at a level. It is for this reason, that sections 13(1) and 13(2) of the SARFEASI Act proceeds on the basis that security interest in the bank/FI needs to be enforced expeditiously without the intervention of the court/tribunal; that liability of the borrower has accrued and on account of default in repayment, the account of the borrower in the books of the bank has become non-performing. Therefore the SARFEASI Act states that the enforcement could take place by non-adjudicatory process and that the said Act removes all fetters under the above circumstances on the rights of the secured creditor.

The Hon'ble Court also examined the object behind insertion of three provisos to section 19(1) of the DRT Act vide amending Act 30 of 2004. The object behind introducing the first proviso and the third proviso to section 19(1) of the DRT Act is to align the provisions of DRT Act, the SARFEASI Act and order XXIII CPC. Let us assume for the sake of argument, that an O.A. is filed in the DRT for recovery of an amount on a term loan, on credit facility and on

hypothecation account. After filing of O.A, on account of non-disposal of the O.A. by the tribunal by heavy backlog, the bank finds that one of the three accounts has become sub- standard/loss, in such case the bank can invoke the NPA Act with or without the permission of the DRT. One cannot lose sight of the fact that even an application for withdrawal/leave takes time for its disposal. With inflation in the economy, value of the pledged property/asset depreciated on a day-to-day basis. If the borrower does not provide additional asset and the value of the asset pledged keeps on falling then to that extent the account becomes non-performing. Therefore, the Bank/FI is required to move under NPA Act expeditiously by taking one of the measures by section 13(4) of the NPA Act. Moreover, Order XXIII CPC is an exception to the common law principle of non-suit, hence the proviso to section 19(1) became a necessity. For the reasons stated above, the Hon'ble Court held that withdrawal of the O.A. pending before the DRT under the DRT Act is not a pre-condition for taking recourse to SARFEASI Act. It is for the bank/FI to exercise its discretion as to cases in which it may apply for leave and in cases where they may not apply for leave to withdraw.

With respect to the second question for determination i.e. whether recourse to take possession of the secured assets of the borrower in terms of section 13(4) of the SARFEASI Act comprehends the power to take actual possession of the immovable property, the Hon'ble Court held that the authorized officer under Rule 8 has greater powers than even a court receiver as security interest in the property already created in favour of the banks/FI. Rule 8 provides that till issuance of the sale certificate under Rule 9, the authorized officer shall take such steps as he deems fit to preserve the secured asset. It is well settled that third party interest are created overnight and in very many cases those third parties take up the defense of being a bona fide purchaser for value without notice. It is these types of disputes which are sought to be avoided by rule 8 read with rule 9 of the 2002 rules. Hence, the Hon'ble Court held that the drawing of dichotomy between symbolic and actual possession does not find place in the scheme of the SARFEASI Act read with the 2002 rules.

While considering the third issue i.e. whether ad valorem court fee prescribed under rule 7 of the DRT (Procedure) Rules, 1993 is payable on an application under section 17(1) of the SARFEASI Act in the absence of any rule framed under the said Act, the Hon'ble court held that as far as the levy of fee is concerned, the terminology makes no difference. In fact, the proviso to section

17(1) indicates that different fees may be prescribed for making an application by the borrower. The reason is obvious. Certain measures taken under section 13(4) like taking over the management of the business of the borrower vis-à-vis the secured creditor taking possession of financial assets have to bear different fees. Each measure is required to be separately charged to the borrower for which different fees could be prescribed. The provision indicates that the tribunal under section 17(1) exercises Original Jurisdiction and therefore, as far as the fees are concerned, the terminology of original or appellate jurisdiction in the context of fees is irrelevant.

In view of the aforesaid grounds, the Honble court dismissed the appeal filed by the borrower- M/s.Transcore and the appeal filed by the banks/FI stands allowed.

3. AUTHORISED OFFICER, INDIAN OVERSEAS BANK & ANOTHER V. ASHOK SAW MILL

The main question which falls for determination before the Hon'ble Supreme Court in Authorised Officer, Indian Overseas Bank v. Ashok Saw Mill53 is whether the DRT would have jurisdiction to consider and adjudicate with regard to post 13(4) events or whether its scope in terms of section 17 of the SARFEASI Act would be confined to the stage contemplated under section 13(4), as contended on behalf of the appellants.

The respondent firm and its sister concern, Ashok Woodworks, availed various loans from the appellant bank which were secured by movable and immovable assets. The loanee firms having defaulted in repayment of the loans and since their accounts became Non-Performing Assets (NPA), the bank initiated action against them under the provisions of the Securitisation and Reconstruction of Financial Assets and Enforcement of Security Interest Act, 2002 (SAREASI Act) and issued separate demand notices to the respondent partnership firm and its sister concern under section 13(2) of SARFEASI Act. As the respondent and its sister concern did not respond to the demand notices, the appellant bank invoked section 13(4) of the SAREASI Act and took possession of the secured assets. The said action of the appellant bank, as also the vires of the SARFEASI Act, were challenged by the respondent firm and its sister concern by way of two separate writ petitions. The said writ petitions were ultimately heard and dismissed with liberty to the respondent firm to approach the Debts Recovery Tribunal. Since, despite such liberty to

the respondent firm did not approach the DRT, the bank take a decision to sell the secured assets of the respondent firm. The same was challenged by the respondent firm in writ petition. After hearing the parties, the High Court refused to grant any interim relief and posted the writ petition for final disposal.

During the pendency of the said writ petition, the respondent firm, along with Ashok Woodworks, filed SARFEASI Application before the DRT at Madurai on the self same cause of action. Despite being informed of the pendency of the writ petition for the self same reliefs, the Tribunal by its order directed the bank to defer the proposed sale. The appellant bank thereupon filed Civil Writ Petition before High Court challenging the filing of the SARFEASI Application.

The same was admitted and all proceedings in the SAREASI Application were stayed. The appellant bank was permitted to open the sealed tenders which it had received pursuant to the sale notice, subject to the condition that the sale effected would be subject to the confirmation of the Court. Pursuant to the said order, the sealed tenders were opened and 3 of the 5 properties were sold and the same was recorded by the DRT. Subsequently, despite the pendency of the review petition, the respondent firm withdrew pending S.A. and filed a fresh S.A. The review petition filed by the bank before the High Court was consequently rendered infructuous and was dismissed. Aggrieved by the said order, bank filed writ appeal, which was dismissed by the Division Bench against which the present appeal preferred before the Hon'ble Supreme Court.

The appellant bank submitted that the scope of the inquiry before the DRT is confined to the action taken by the secured creditor under section 13(4) of the SARFEASI Act and the subsequent action taken to bring the secured assets to sale or to transfer the interest therein in any manner whatsoever, could not be made the subject-matter of inquiry before the DRT. In other words, the jurisdiction of the Tribunal under section 17(3) would have to be confined to any action taken by the secured creditor in taking possession of the secured assets under sub-section

(4) of section 13 and not in regard to any subsequent steps which the secured creditor may take to dispose off the secured assets in accordance with the provisions of the Act.

The intention of the Legislature is clear that while the Bank's/FI's have been vested with stringent powers for recovery of their dues, safeguards have also been provided for rectifying any error or wrongful use of such powers by vesting the DRT with authority after conducting an

adjudication into the matter to declare any such action invalid and also to restore possession even though possession may have been made over to the transferee. The consequences of the authority vested in DRT under sub-section (3) of section 17 necessarily implies that the DRT is entitled to question the action taken by the secured creditor and the transactions entered into by virtue of section 13(A) of the Act. The Legislature by including sub-section (3) in section 17 has gone to the extent of vesting the DRT with authority to even set aside a transaction including sale and to restore possession to the borrower in appropriate cases. Resultantly, the submissions advanced by the appellant bank that the DRT has no jurisdiction to deal with a post- 13-(4) situation, cannot be accepted. The law contemplates that the action taken by a secured creditor in terms of section 13- (4) is open to scrutiny and cannot only be set aside but even the status quo ante can be restored by the DRT. With these findings, the Hon'ble Court see no reason to interfere with the judgment and order of the High Court and the appeal is accordingly dismissed.

4.   UNITED BANK OF INDIA V SATYAWATI TONDON AND OTHERS

The Hon'ble Supreme Court of India in its judgement on July 26, 2010 in United Bank of India v Satyawati Tondon and others 54 held that despite repeated pronouncement of Supreme Court, the High Court's continue to ignore the availability of statutory remedies under the DRT Act and SARFAESI Act and exercise jurisdiction under Article 226 for passing orders which have serious adverse impact on the right of Banks and other financial institutions to recover their dues.

In the case on hand, the appellant Bank sanctioned a term loan in favour M/s.Pawan Color Lab and the respondent no.1 gave guarantee for repayment of the loan and mortgaged her property by deposit of title deeds. The appellant Bank issued notice to respondents under section 13(2) of the SARFAESI Act. Upon receipt of the notice, respondent no.1 offered to pay a sum of Rs.18 lakhs for settlement of the loan account, but the appellant Bank did not accept the offer and filed an application under Section 14 of the SARFAESI Act, which was allowed by the District Magistrate/Collector. Thereafter, the appellant Bank issued notice to respondent under Section 13(4) of the SARFEASI Act.

Faced with the imminent threat of losing the mortgaged property, respondent no.1 filed Civil Mis.Writ Petition praying for an order restraining appellant Bank from taking coercive action in pursuance of the notices issued under section 13(2) and (4) and the order passed by District

Magistrate/Collector. The Division Bench of the High Court did not advert to the appellant's plea that the writ petition should not be entertained because an alternative remedy was available to the writ petitioner under section 17 of the SARFAESI Act and passed order restraining the appellant from taking action in furtherance of notice issued under section 13(4) of the SARFAESI Act on the ground that Bank should have proceeded against the borrower and exhausted all the remedies before proceeding against the guarantor.

While dealing with this Special Leave Petition preferred by the appellant Bank, the Hon'ble Supreme Court of India observed that the question whether the appellant Bank could have issued notices to guarantor and filed application under section 14 of the SARFAESI Act without first initiating action against the borrower for recovery of the outstanding dues is no longer res integra.

The Hon'ble Supreme Court held that the High Court completely misdirected itself in assuming that the appellant could not have initiated action against the guarantor without making efforts for recovery of its dues from the borrower. Further, if the guarantor had any tangible grievance against the notice issued under section 13(4) or action taken under section 14, then the guarantor could have availed remedy by filing an application under section 17(1) of SARFAESI Act. It is thus evident that the remedies available to an aggrieved person under the SARFAESI Act are both expeditious and effective. Unfortunately, the High Court overlooked the settled law that it will ordinarily not entertain a petition under Article 226 of the Constitution if an effective remedy is available to the aggrieved person and that this rule applies with greater rigour in matters involving recovery of taxes, cess, fees, other types of public money and the dues of banks and other financial institutions. While dealing with the petitions involving challenge to the action taken for recovery of public dues, etc., the High Court must keep in mind that the legislations enacted by Parliament and State Legislatures for recovery of such dues are code unto themselves in as much as they not only contain comprehensive procedure for recovery of the dues but also envisage constitution of quasijudicial bodies for redressal of the grievance of any aggrieved person. Therefore, in all such cases,High Court must insist that before availing remedy under Article 226 of the Constitution, a person must exhaust the remedies available under the relevant statute.

The Hon'ble Court held that in cases relating to recovery of the dues of banks, financial institutions and secured creditors, stay granted by the High Court would have serious adverse impact on the financial health of such bodies/institutions, which ultimately prove detrimental to the economy of the nation. Therefore, the High Court should be extremely careful and circumspect in exercising its discretion to grant stay in such matters. In City and Industrial Development Corporation v. Dosu Aardeshir Bhiwandiwala and others55 (2009) 1 SCC 168, the Hon'ble Supreme Court highlighted the parameters which are required to be kept in view by the High Court while exercising jurisdiction under Article 226 of the Consitution. The High Court while exercising its jurisdiction under Article 226 is duty – bound to consider:-

Whether the adjudication of writ petition involves any complex and disputed questions of facts and whether they can be satisfactorily resolved;

- Whether the petition reveals all material facts;
- Whether the petitioner has any alternative or effective remedy for the resolution of the dispute;
- Whether the person invoking the jurisdiction is guilty of unexplained delay and laches;
- Whether it is ex facie barred by any laws of limitation;
- Whether the grant of relief is against public policy or barred by any valid law; and host of other factors.

After analyzing the aforesaid parameters and the factual matrix of the case, the Hon'ble Supreme Court held that the High Court was not at all justified in injuncting the appellant from taking action in furtherance of notice issued under Section 13(4) of the Act. The Hon'ble Court further held that it is a matter of serious concern that despite repeated pronouncement of the Supreme Court, the High Court's continue to ignore the availability of statutory remedies under the DRT Act and SARFAESI Act and exercise jurisdiction under Article 226 for passing orders which have serious adverse impact on the right of banks and other financial institutions to recover their dues. While disposing off the Special Leave Petition, the Hon'ble Supreme Court declared that it hopes and trusts that in future the High Courts will exercise their discretion in such matters with greater caution, care and circumspection.

5.   EUREKA FORBES LIMITED VS. ALLAHABAD BANK AND ORS

The question whether DRT has jurisdiction to entertain and decide the claim of the Bank against a person who is neither a borrower nor any kind of privity of contract exists between the Bank and that person? is discussed and decided by the Hon'ble Supreme Court of India in its judgement delivered on 03.05.2010 in Eureka Forbes Limited Vs. Allahabad Bank and Ors[49] Ahead of discussing the legal nuances involved in this case, it would be appropriate to familiarize with the factual matrix of the case. A brief description of the factual matrix of the case is given below:-

The appellant company M/s.Eureka Forbes Ltd entered into an agreement with respondents, granting license in their favour to use premises along with the plant and machinery as well as their trade mark. The respondents had availed certain cash credit facility and had hypothecated their raw materials, semi-finished products to Allahabad Bank. Since the respondents failed to pay the license fee for the use and occupation of the premises, goods, etc they requested the appellant company to take over the possession of the premises along with the closing stock lying therein. Meanwhile, the respondent Bank wrote to the respondent raising an issue as to how the possession of the stocks and machinery was given to the appellant company since they had a charge over the movable assets.

The Bank filed suit against the appellant company and respondents for recovery of Bank's dues. The appellant company filed a written statement making a preliminary objection that there was no privity of contract between the Bank and the appellant and the appellant is not a borrower of the Bank and had no dealings with them as such, the suit was barred for mis- joinder of parties and in fact no suit could lie against the present appellant. It was stated on merits that neither they were aware of any transaction between the Bank and respondents nor of any charge over the machinery and equipment etc. Later on, when the Recovery Act came into force, the suit stands transferred to DRT. The appellant did not appear before the DRT and an exparte judgment was passed against the appellant. The appellant company filed an application for condonation of delay and for recalling the ex-parte order. Consequent upon the dismissal of the application for condonation of delay, the appellant filed an appeal before the DRAT. While setting aside the ex-

[49] 56Eureka Forbes Limited Vs. Allahabad Bank and Ors, Civil Appeal No.4029 of 2010(Arising out of SLP © No.3883 of 2008).

parte decree, the Appellate Tribunal directed the respondent bank to refund the sum appropriated from the appellant company in terms of the previous order together with interest at the lending rate.

The respondent Bank challenged the order of the DRAT under Article 227 of the Constitution before the Single Judge of the Kolkata High Court, but the order of DRAT was restored by the Single Judge of the High Court. Aggrieved by which, the Bank preferred the appeal before the Division Bench of Kolkata High Court, which by its order dismissed the appeal and sustained the order of the Single Judge. Again aggrieved by the said order, the Bank preferred Special Leave Petition before the Hon'ble Supreme Court.

The Hon'ble Supreme Court of India held that the entire case of the parties' hinges on the ambit and scope of the provisions of section 2(g) of the Debt Recovery Act, which defines "debt". The section 2(g) of the Debt Recovery Act defined debt and it means any liability(inclusive of interest) which is claimed as due from any person by a bank or a financial institution or by a consortium of banks or financial institutions during the course of any business activity undertaken by the bank or the financial institution or the consortium under any law for the time being in force, in cash or otherwise, whether secured or unsecured, or assigned, or whether payable under a decree or order of any civil court or any arbitration award or otherwise or under a mortgage and subsisting on, and legally recoverable on, the date of the application.

The Hon'ble Supreme Court held that the plain reading of the section 2(g) suggests that legislature has used a general expression in contra distinction to specific, restricted or limited expression. This obviously means that, the legislature intended to give wider meaning to the provisions. Larger area of jurisdiction was intended to be covered under this provision so as to ensure attainment of the legislative object i.e. expeditious recovery and providing provisions for taking such measures which would prevent the wastage of securities available with the banks and financial institutions. The expression 'any person' shows that the framers do not wish to restrict the same in its ambit or application. The legislature has not intended to restrict to the relationship of a creditor or debtor alone. General terms, therefore, have been used by the legislature to give the provision a wider and liberal meaning. These are generic or general terms. Therefore, it will be difficult for the court, even on cumulative reading of the provision, to hold that the expression should be given a narrower or restricted meaning. What will be more in consonance with the

purpose and object of the Act is to give this expression a general meaning on its plain language rather than apply unnecessary emphasis or narrow the scope and interpretation of these provisions, as they are likely to frustrate the very object of the Act. The Hon'ble Court held that in the case in hand, there cannot be any dispute that the expression "debt" has to be given the widest amplitude to mean any liability which is alleged as due from any person by a bank during the course of any business activity undertaken by the bank either in cash or otherwise, whether secured or unsecured, whether payable under a decree or order of any court or otherwise and legally recoverable on the date of the application.

After careful consideration of the factual matrix and legal issues involved in this case, the Hon'ble Supreme Court held that there is no dispute of the fact that goods had been hypothecated to the Bank and in spite of complete knowledge of this fact, appellant company went on to sell the goods. The Bank had been negligent and to some extent, irresponsible in invoking its rights and taking appropriate remedy in accordance with law. The Hon'ble Court declared that mere irresponsibility, on the part of the Bank, would not wipe out the rights of the Bank in law. Without the consent of the Bank, no person can utilize the hypothecated goods for his own benefit or sale by the borrower or any person connected thereto. It is nobody's case that the Bank had consented to such sale. Physical domain over the hypothecated goods is no way a sine qua non for enforcing Bank's rights against the borrower. It was obligatory upon the appellant to deal with the goods only with the leave and permission of the Bank. Absence of such consent in writing would obviously result in breach of Bank's rights.

The Hon'ble Court held that the documentary and oral evidence on record clearly established that the Bank has raised a financial claim upon the principal debtor as well as upon the person who had intermeddled or at least dealt with the charged goods without any authority in law.

The respondents and the appellant have acted together while disposing off the hypothecated goods, and now, they cannot be permitted to turn back to argue that since the goods have been sold, liability cannot be fastened upon them. The legal maxim nullus commodum capere potest de injuria sua has a clear mandate of law that, a person who by manipulation of a process frustrates the legal rights of others, should not be permitted to take advantage of his wrong or manipulations.

The court further observed that in the event when a party which had pledged or mortgaged properties in favour of the Bank, transferred such properties in favour of a third party, the Bank is entitled to takes action under the provisions of the DRT Act. Otherwise, it would tantamount to travesty of justice and would frustrate the very legislative object and intent behind the provisions of the DRT Act. The Hon'ble Court held that the claim of the Bank relatable to the hypothecated goods was well within the jurisdiction of the Tribunal exercising its power under Section 17 of the DRT Act.

The Hon'ble court further held that the facts of the case indicate definite negligence and callousness on the part of the concerned officers/officials in the Bank. The legislative object of expeditious recovery of all public dues and due protection of security available with the Bank to ensure pre-payments of debts cannot be achieved when the officers/officials of the Bank act in such a callous manner. Accordinlgy, the Hon'ble court allowed the appeal and directed the appellants to pay to the respondent Bank a sum of Rs.9,63,975/- with interest to the date of actual realization. The Hon'ble court also directed the chairman of the Allahabad

Bank to examine this case in the light of the negligence and callousness on the part of the concerned officers/officials in the Bank and take appropriate action against erring officers/officials in accordance with law.

6. INDIAN BANK vs. BLUE JAGGERS ESTATES LTD AND OTHERS

The Hon'nble Supreme Court of India in its judgement delivered in Indian Bank Vs. Blue Jaggers Estates Ltd and others[50] on 09.08.2010 held that doctrine of unconscionable contract cannot be invoked for frustrating the action initiated by the appellant Bank for recovery of its dues. Of late, defaulting borrowers are using court process for frustrating the action initiated by the Bank under the provisions of Securitisation and Reconstruction of Financial Assets and Enforcement of Security Interest Act, 2002 for recovery of its dues. The Hon'ble Supreme Court of India held that the appeals filed by the default borrowers in this case are illustrative of how a defaulting borrower can use the court process for frustrating the action initiated by the Bank for recovery of its dues. The appellant – bank sanctioned loan to N.S.Investments, a partnership firm and the account of N.S.Investments was declared as non-performing asset and the respondent no.1 Blue Jaggers Estate Ltd took over the assets and liabilities of N.S.Investments. Since the

[50] Indian Bank Vs. Blue Jaggers Estates Ltd and others, reported in 2010(4) Current Tamilnadu Cases (SC)

respondents failed to clear the outstanding dues, the appellant filed an application under Sec.19 of the Recovery of Debts Due to Banks and Financial Institutions Act, 1993. During the pendency of original application, the parties signed Joint Memo of Compromise whereby the appellant bank agreed to accept an amount of Rs.153.50 lakhs towards full and final settlement of its claim. The parties also agreed that in case of non-compliance of any of the conditions, the Original Application shall stand decreed.

In the meanwhile, the appellant Bank issued notice under section 13(2) of the SARFEASI Act. The respondents filed objections under section 13(3-A) of the SARFEASI Act and claimed that during the pendency of the recovery proceedings instituted under the DRT Act, the appellant cannot invoke the provisions of the Act. The appellant Bank did not accede to the request of the respondents and issued notice under section 13(4) of the SARFEASI Act for taking possession of the mortgaged properties. Faced with the imminent threat of sale of the mortgaged properties, the respondents filed application under section 17 of the SARFEASI Act. With the sole object of delaying final adjudication of the application filed by them, the respondents filed three interlocutory applications.

The Ld.DRT dismissed section 17 application filed by the respondents. The respondents challenged the order of the Ld.DRT by filing an appeal under section 18 of the SARFEASI Act. The Debts Recovery Appellate Tribunal granted interim stay subject to the condition of deposit of Rs.3 crores in two equal installments. The writ petition was dismissed by the Divison Bench of Madras High Court. Since the respondents did not comply with the order passed by the Appellate Tribunal, the authorized officer of the appellant bank auctioned some of the mortgaged properties. Thereafter, the respondents filed two writ petitions, one for quashing the order of the Appellate Tribunal and another for issue of a mandamus to the Tribunal to dispose of the Original Application. While disposing off the writ petitions, the Hon'ble division bench of the High Court not only set aside the interim order passed by the Appellate Tribunal, but also declared that as a result of sale of the property worth Rs.5 crores, the requirement of deposit of Rs.3 crores stands satisfied.

Aggrieved by the order of division bench of the Hon'ble High Court, the appellant Bank approached the Hon'ble Supreme Court of India and argued that the Division Bench of the High Court did not have the jurisdiction to nullify the conditional interim order passed by the

Appellate Tribunal as the writ petition filed against that order was dismissed by the High Court and the special leave petition was dismissed by the Supreme Court. Further, the High Court committed serious error by taking note of the bids given at the auction for the purpose of relieving the respondents of their statutory obligation to deposit 50% of the debts due.

The Hon'ble Supreme Court held that the respondents cannot be allowed to indirectly question correctness of the order of the Appellate Tribunal to deposit Rs.3 crores because the respondent's challenge to that order was negatived by the High Court and Supreme Court. Another argument of the respondent that the rate of interest is unconscionable, expropriatory and contrary to law merits rejection because at no stage the respondents had questioned the terms on which loan and other financial facilities were extended by the appellant. The fact of the matter is that the respondents had signed the agreement with open eyes and agreed to abide by the terms on which the loan, etc was offered by the appellant. Therefore, the doctrine of unconscionable contract cannot be invoked for frustrating the action initiated by the appellant for recovery of its dues. The respondent's accusation that the appellant bank had not treated them fairly sans credibility. It is the respondents who had failed to repay the outstanding dues. It is further observed that court cannot lose sight of the fact that the bank is a trustee of public funds. The Banks cannot compromise the public interest for benefitting private individuals. Those who take loan and avail financial facilities from the bank are duty bound to repay the amount strictly in accordance with the terms of the contract. Any lapse in such matters has to be viewed seriously and the bank is not only entitled but duty bound to recover the amount by adopting all legally permissible methods. The Parliament enacted the Act because it was found that legal mechanism available till then was wholly insufficient for recovery of the outstanding dues of banks and financial institutions. Accordingly, the civil appeal filed by the appellant Bank was allowed by the Hon'ble Supreme Court and the impugned order of the High Court was set aside insofar as it declares that the direction given by the Appellate Tribunal to the respondents to deposit Rs.3 crores stands complied.

7. ICICI BANK V. SHANTI DEVI SHARMA AND OTHERS

The judgement of the Hon'ble Supreme Court in this case is an eye opener to the Bank/Financial Institutions who are not complying with the rules and regulations for recovery of dues from the borrowers. While dealing with the aforesaid criminal appeal arising out of SLP (crl) no.4935 of

2006, decided on 15.05.2008, between ICICI BANK V. SHANTI DEVI SHARMA AND

OTHERS58, the Hon'ble Supreme Court of India has reminded financial Institutions that they are bound by law. The recovery of loans or seizure of vehicles can only be done through legal means. The Hon'ble Court further reminded that we live in a civilized country and are governed by the rule of law.

The respondent in this criminal appeal had filed a criminal writ petition in the Delhi High Court, seeking a writ of mandamus to direct the Commissioner of Police to take action against the ICICI Bank. The respondent alleged that her son committed suicide as a result of the manner in which the Bank's recovery agents had repossessed her son's motorcycle. In the first information report, the respondent alleged that the recovery agents repossessed the vehicle in the presence of his friends who ridiculed him for having lost the motorcycle. The deceased son of the respondent finally broke down before his wife and allegedly stated that he had never faced such a humiliation /disgrace in his entire life and ultimately hung himself to death. To ascertain the veracity of these assertions in the first information report, the Hon'ble High Court orders the police to file reports as to the status of the investigation against the Bank. The

Hon'ble High Court reviewed the status reports and directed the Investigating Officer to conclude

the investigation into the matter as expeditiously as possible and take necessary action against those who may be found guilty of abetting the deceased to commit suicide. In addition Hon'ble High Court also stated in the order that:

"Para 1:...... the vehicle for which the loan was taken was repossessed by the musclemen employed by ICICI Bank".

"Pare 3 the proximate cause of death of the deceased that led him to commit suicide was on

account of humiliation caused by the Bank people from where loan was taken by him".

"Para 4:...... the modus operandi employed by the Bank like ICICI for realisation of their loan amount and for recovering the possession of the vehicle against which loans are given is extra

legal and by no stretch of imagination they can be permitted to employ muscleman and goons for recovery of their dues even from defaulting party".

The appellant Bank being aggrieved by the observations made by the High Court as given in paras 1, 3 & 4 asked the High Court to clarify or delete paras 1, 3 & 4. However, the High Court declined to expunge the impugned observations but clarified that any observation made against ICICI Bank shall not influence or affect the proceedings, if any, taken against the said Bank or its employees.

Not satisfied with the clarification given by the High Court, ICICI Bank preferred the instant appeal. However in the appeal, the Hon'ble Supreme Court reiterates the stand taken by the High Court and held that neither the High Court order nor the observations made herein are to influence the investigation.

The Hon'ble Supreme Court also took this opportunity to remind the financial Institutions

CONCLUSION

From the study conducted it has been ascertained that the cases get delayed inordinately in a Debt Recovery Tribunal much against the spirit and motive of its very establishment. Banks have expressed their dissatisfaction with the system that was instituted to ensure speedy recovery. The number of claims in litigation is quite large and changes should be made urgently to revamp the existing model. Unless the system is overhauled, the rate of pendency at the Tribunal will rise unrestrained. Such a state of affairs will seriously put the banking system in doldrums.

The functioning of Debt Recovery Tribunals (DRTs), created to help financial institutions recover dues speedily without being subjected to the lengthy procedures of usual civil courts, appears to cause more pain than gain for banks. Consider this: The amount recovered from cases decided in 2013-14 under DRTs was Rs 30,950 crore, while the outstanding value of debt sought to be recovered was Rs 2,36,600 crore. In other words, recovery was only 13 per cent of the amount at stake. Also, while the law indicates that cases before DRTs must be disposed off in six months, only about a fourth of the cases pending at the beginning of the year were disposed during the year. *"The functioning of DRTs needs to improve to ensure bank are able to recover their existing loans and offer fresh advances at cheaper rates. In the current scheme of things, there is no mechanism in place to ensure that the tribunal disposes the case in a timely manner. There is a strong need to bring in more accountability for the DRT,"* said Shashwat Sharma, partner (Management Consulting), KPMG in India. One problem is the small number of DRTs and Debt Recovery Appellate Tribunals, where judgments of DRTs can be appealed. While there are 33 DRTs, there are only five Debt Recovery Appellate Tribunals in the country. *"There is certainly a need for more number of DRTs. The biggest challenge, it appears, is their ability to deal with a subject with speed. The system that was designed is clearly not working. Probably, there should be a feedback mechanism and people involved with DRTs should be encouraged to point out the areas of pain,"* said Ashvin Parekh,

Managing Partner at Ashvin Parekh Advisory Services. Deepak Haria, Senior Director at Deloitte in India, echoed a similar view. *"The challenge is that our judicial system is both clogged and inadequate in infrastructure, which slows down any redressal. Recovery can be speeded up only when there is a fixed time-frame for all disposals, and realisation of assets could be speeded up by having special courts to deal with such recoveries,"* he said. *The functioning of DRTs is also keeping the* **Reserve Bank** *of* **India (RBI)** *worried. "If bankers cannot get their money back, they are not going to give you loans at cheap price. So, making sure debt recovery tribunals work better, making sure that you*

don't have excess number of stays, excess number of appeals — that is what we need to focus on," RBI Governor Raghuram Rajan said following the central bank's fifth bi-monthly monetary policy review. Experts suggest that the law should be strengthened to ensure mandatory time-bound disposal of cases. Also, performance indicators of the adjudicating officer could be used to improve the efficiency of the system. A few recommended that stay petitions should be analysed before being accepted as there have been instances where advocates exploit the loopholes of the Act and plead for stays, leading to piling up of cases.

As to the suggestions to improve the *debt recovery scenario in the country* it is recommended that the time bound disposal of cases though the Court has to dispose an order application within six months, and a stay application within two months from the date of its admission, this has not been followed by the Tribunals in India in many situations. The government has to make sure that time-bound disposal of the cases is done mandatorily by adding the clause in the Act and making it a law. Even though the *SARFAESI* Act has mandated the Debt Recovery Tribunals to settle the Original Applications within six months, this is not obeyed strictly. Efforts have to be taken to ensure this.

SUGGESTIONS AND RECOMMENDATIONS

The suggestions and recommendations of the research are can be grouped into three categories:-

The suggestions and recommendations pertaining to the amendments in the Acts are given under the title suggestions and recommendations in legal provisions. The suggestions and recommendations pertaining to the instructions from the regulators such as the Reserve Bank of India and Ministry of Finance are given under the title suggestions and recommendations in regulatory framework. The suggestions and recommendations pertaining to the policy guidelines from the various bodies of the Government are given under the title suggestions and recommendations in policy matters. The suggestions and recommendations under the various heads are given pictorially in the charts along with the detailed description. The suggestions and the recommendations are based on the detailed research and analysis of the data collected from various stake holders.

SUGGESTIONS TO AMEND THE PROVISIONS OF SECURITISATION AND RECONSTRUCTION OF FINANCIAL ASSETS AND ENFORCEMENT OF SECURITY INTEREST ACT, 2002

1. Amendment in the definition of the term "authorised officer" in rule 2 (a) of the security interest (enforcement) rules, 2002.
2. A new provision may be incorporated after section 35 in the sarfaesi act so as to give priority of charges created by secured creditor
3. Amendment may be brought in section 30 of sarfaesi act to empower the court to take cognizance of any offence upon a complaint by authorised officer
4. New provision may be incorporated in rule 8 of security interest (enforcement) rules, to grant first right of purchase to

borrower/guarantor

5.   New provision may be incorporated in rule 8 (6) of security interest rules to publish photographs of borrowers/ guarantor

6.   Section 14 of sarfasei act may be amended to insert the word chief judicial magistrate

7.   New provision may be inserted in section 14 of sarfaesi act for timely disposal of the application

8.   Rule 8 (5) (d) of security interest (enforcement) rules, 2002 may be modified to insert word "eauction

9.   Rule 9 (4) of the security interest (enforcement) rules, 2002 may be modified so as to clarify the words "between the parties

SUGGESTIONS TO AMEND THE PROVISIONS OF SECURITISATION AND RECONSTRUCTION OF FINANCIAL ASSETS AND ENFORCEMENT OF SECURITY INTEREST ACT, 2002

I.   Amendment in the definition of the term "authorised officer" in rule 2 (a) of the security interest (enforcement) rules, 2002.

During the course of the research, it is found that the authorized officers are not exercising their powers judiciously and with fairness. Hence, there is a need to streamline the actions of the authorised officers strictly in compliance with the provisions of the SARFAESI Act. The authorised officers must be provided with proper training for enabling them to discharge their quasi-judicial functions. It must be ensured that the officials who are acting as authorised officers must undergo training or qualify the test so as to eligible themselves as authorised officers. In this connection, the Indian Banking Association in association with the member banks can organize a training course for the authorised officers of all the Banks. The Indian Banking Association has commenced a training course for the recovery agents. In the same line, Indian Banking Association can initiate a training course for the authorised officers of all banks. The course can be arranged in such a way as to include the provisions of the SARFAESI Act, DRT Act, Banking Code and Standard Board of India, Responsibility of Lenders, etc.

II.   A NEW PROVISION MUST BE INCORPORATE AFTER SECTION 35 IN THE SARFAESI ACT SO AS TO GIVE PRIORITY OF CHARGES CREATED BY THE SECURED CREDITOR DURING ENFORCEMENT

In order to make the provisions of the Sarfaesi Act more effective, it is suggested that the Banks should be given the first right over defaulters assets to exercise the same, without being interrupted by the tax authorities. The idea is to make use of the overriding nature of the Sarfaesi Act to virtually ensure that a lender gets to recover dues from a defaulter before other. One way of doing this is to give priority to those who have registered their charge with the Central

Registry established by the Central Government in recovery of dues. In practice, tax authorities and municipal corporations often attach the assets of a defaulting company beforehand, which comes in the way of Banks in recovering their dues.

Under the provisions of the Income Tax Act, Central Excise Act and like, the concerned officers have got power to attach the assets. The provision must be made in Sarfaesi Act to give priority rights to the secured creditors for recovery of money. The registration of charge needs to be with the Central Registry of Securitisation Asset Reconstuction and Security Interest of India (Cersai) set up to eliminate instances of multiple lending. The principle of first to register a lien on the assets of the defaulting companies can be adopted as the guiding principle. These changes to the Sarfaesi Act will be a huge leapfrog in terms of reforms in this area and will also be in tune with international best practices followed by UK, US, Australia and Cananda.

The enactment of the Sarfaesi Act has clearly established that creditors rights need to be protected. But, the object of the Central law may be defeated on account of various State Governments enacting laws giving priority to claims of the State

Government towards arrears of sales tax and other dues of Government over secured debts. Validity of such State legislation's needs to be considered in the context of inconsistent provisions contained in Union Laws such as the Sarfaesi Act, 2002 and Recovery of Debts due to Banks and Financial Institutions Act, 1993.

The provisions which give priority to the claims of the sovereign over that of the secured creditors is a cause of concern. The law should be amended so as to provide that the priority of charge for state dues should not operate in respect of prior mortgages created in favour of secured creditors. It is also worthwhile to have a common legislation to deal with the creation and registration of security interests irrespective of the nature of security and its location. The Union Government can also take steps to extend the law to other creditors such as non-banking finance companies and thereby encourage lending activities in the financial market.

The Section 35 of the SARFAESI Act state that the provisions of the Act shall have effect, notwithstanding anything inconsistent therewith contained in any other law for the time being in force or any instrument having effect by virtue of any such law. However, there is no provision which provide priority rights to the Banks of the security charge created in their favour in case of enforcement of SARFAESI proceedings. Hence, a new section may be incorporated subsequent to Section 35 detailing about the priority right of Banks in case of enforcement of security under the SARFAESI Act by taking into account the date of creation of security as cutoff date.

OTHER SUGGESTIONS AND RECOMMENDATIONS:

1. The application of the Sarfaesi Act can be made applicable to all secured creditors and not only to the banks and FI's.
2. Segregate provisions relating to Securitisation from the Act and enact a separate law for securitisation of financial assets.
3. The provisions of Sarfaesi Act can extend to financial leases, hire purchase and sales on credit transactions.
4. In cases of sale by private treaty under the provisions of the SARFAESI Act, a notice shall be given to the borrower to obtain a better offer within the time specified failing which the secured creditor can proceed to sell the property.
5. In cases where the borrower has been given notice of 30 days for public auction of secured assets under the provisions of the SARFAESI Act and if such auction fails, any subsequent auction can be held with shorter notice of 15 days instead of 30 days.
6. Amend Section 17 of the SARFAESI Act empowering DRTs to decide rights of lessees or tenants or any other person claiming rights in the mortgaged properties and pass orders to protect their rights. The SARFAESI Act also needs to be amended to declare that notwithstanding anything contained in any other law, the borrower cannot sell, lease or deal with any property over which security interest is created without the consent of the secured creditor, except sale of its products or services.
7. In terms of Section 15 of the SARFAESI Act, the Banks have been empowered to take over the management of the borrower company whose assets have mortgaged with the Bank in case of default. However, in cases where the assets of the company is not mortgaged with Bank, there is no specific provisions to enable secured creditors to induct new members on the boards of defaulting borrower companies and attach assets that had not been pledged. If the Banks were given powers to induct persons with responsibility to run the company, it would be more professional and fair.

Bibliography

Anant, T.C.A, Singh, Jaivir, Structuring Regulation, 2006, Constitutional and Legal Frame in India, Economic and Political Weekly 41(2), 121-127.

Bhue, G., N. Prabhala, and P. Tantri, 2016, "Creditor Rights and Relationship Banking: Evidence from a Policy Experiment," CAFRAL Working Paper.

Batra, Sumant, 2003, Asian Recovery: Progress and Pitfalls: The Position of India, World Bank Global Forum on Insolvency Risk Management (Washington DC).

Dubey, G.S, 2013, An Introduction to the Recovery of Debts Due to Banks and Financial Institutions Act, 1993 – A study, Chartered Account Practice Journal

September 16 – September 30, 684 – 692.

Gopalan Radhakrishnan, Mukherjee Abhiroop, Singh Manpreet, 2014, Do Debt Contract Enforcement Costs Affects Financing and Asset Structure?, Working Paper, Washington University and Hong Kong University of Science and Technology.

Gormley, Todd, Nandini, Gupta, Jha, Anand, 2011, Corporate Bankruptcy and Creditor Incentives, Working paper, University of Pennsylvania, Indiana University and Texas A&M International University.

Government of India, The Recovery of Debts Due to Banks and Financial Institutions Act, 1993, Government of India Publications: New Delhi, India.

Government of India, Securitisation and Reconstruction of Financial Assets and Enforcement of Security Interest (SARFAESI) Act, 2002, Government of India Publications: New Delhi, India.

Government of India, Sick Industrial Company (Special Provisions) Act, 1985, Government of India Publications: New Delhi, India.

Government of India, The Enforcement of Security Interest and Recovery of Debts Laws (Amendment) Act, 2012, Government of India Publications: New Delhi, India.

Kang, Nimrit, and Nitin Nayar, 2004, The Evolution of Corporate Bankruptcy Law in India, ICRA Bulletin, Money and Finance, Oct 03 – March 04, 37-58.

Lilenfeld-Toal, Ulf, Mukherjee, Dilip, and Visaria, Sujata, 2012, The Distributive Impact of Reforms in Credit Enforcement: Evidence from Indian Debt Recovery Tribunals, Econometrica 80(2), 497-558.

Sharma, Nilesh, and Sandeep Gupta, 2013, The Restructuring Review, Law Business Review 6th Edition, 163-175.

Unny, Mukund, 2011, A Study of the Effectiveness of remedies available for banks in a Debt Recovery Tribunal – A case study of Ernakulam DRT, Working Paper Series, Centre for Public Policy Research, 1-35.

Vig, Vikrant, 2013, Access to Collateral and Corporate Debt Structure: Evidence from a Natural Experiment, Journal of Finance 68(3), 881-928.

Visaria, Sujata, 2009, Legal Reforms and Loan Repayment: The Microeconomic Impact of Debt Recovery Tribunals in India, American Economic Journal: Applied Economics 1, 59-81.

Zwieten, Kristin, 2014, Corporate Rescue in India: The Influence of the Courts, Journal of Corporate Law Studies, Vol. 1, 2015.

Contents